ARKANA

The Legend of the Sons of God

T. C. Lethbridge, who died in 1971, was an archaeologist, psychic researcher, dowser, explorer. He was for thirty years Director of Excavations for the Cambridge Antiquarian Society and for the University Museum of Archaeology and Ethnology. He was on three Arctic expeditions, several Hebridean exploratory expeditions and two voyages to the Baltic in square-rigged sailing ships. He was also, as Colin Wilson wrote, 'one of the most remarkable and original minds in parapsychology'. His other books include *Gogmagog*, *The Power of the Pendulum*, *The Monkey's Tail*, *A Step in the dark* and *Witches*.

T. C. Lethbridge

The Legend of the Sons of God

A Fantasy?

ARKANA

ARKANA

Published by the Penguin Group
27 Wrights Lane, London W8 5TZ, England
Viking Penguin Inc., 40 West 23rd Street, New York, New York 10010, USA
Penguin Books Australia Ltd, Ringwood, Victoria, Australia
Penguin Books Canada Ltd, 2801 John Street, Markham, Ontario, Canada L3R 1B4
Penguin Books (NZ) Ltd, 182–190 Wairau Road, Auckland 10, New Zealand

Penguin Books Ltd, Registered Offices: Harmondsworth, Middlesex, England

First published by Routledge & Kegan Paul Ltd 1972
Published by Arkana 1990
1 3 5 7 9 10 8 6 4 2

Printed and bound in Great Britain by
Cox & Wyman Ltd, Reading, Berks.

Contents

Introduction ix

One 1

Two 25

Three 35

Four 47

Five 56

Six 64

Seven 73

Eight 81

Nine 90

Ten 99

Eleven 108

Figures

		page
1	Sketch and plan of Callanish avenues and circle	9
2	Sketch of part of the circle at Stonehenge	10
3	Sketch of the Merry Maidens near Lamorna	14
4	A. Small West Greenland umiak; B. Suggested method of transporting stones	17
5	Sketchmap of places mentioned in the text in connection with old stone monuments	20
6	Sketches of two Christian wheel-headed crosses near the Merry Maidens	23
7	Reconstruction of an Easter Island statue	37
8	Finds from cremation urns at the cemetery excavated at Lackford	39
9	Sun discs from Scandinavian early Bronze Age rock engravings	67
10	Sketches of craters on the moon	91

Introduction

My wife had nearly finished typing this book when a friend, Group Captain Guy Knocker, sent me a copy of Erich von Daniken's *Chariots of the Gods?* The two books were so similar in many ways that I felt tempted to destroy my version. However, I saw that there were points of difference and that this was an interesting example of the often observed phenomenon of a particular idea occurring to people in different parts of the world at the same time, just as if it had been put into their heads from outside. The best known case, of course, is that of Darwin and Wallace who shared the Theory of Evolution in 1859.

As it happened I had been interested in the problem of who were 'the sons of God' for many years and had sought enlightenment from archaeologists, anthropologists and theologians at Cambridge and elsewhere without getting the slightest satisfaction. Nobody knew the answer. If von Daniken's ideas and mine have any sense in them, nobody could have known the answer before the present generation, for travel to other planets was unthinkable. Since this has now changed, it is obviously time that people did begin to think about these matters which clearly affect the whole meaning of life on earth. Is there more than one species of Man and is he found on many different planets?

Of course I could not be expected to know the answer, but it is worth throwing a stone into the pool to see what then moves in it.

My wife, who is my great helper and best critic as well as carrying the burden of typing it all out, seems to think that I am not crazy in formulating these ideas and so I will throw the stone and hope for the best.   T.C.L.

One

When I was still at Cambridge and digging for the museum and the Antiquarian Society, I happened to find a giant figure, or rather three giant figures, cut in the turf of the chalk hill at Wandlebury, some three miles to the south of the town. About half of the students of British archaeology realized what they were: the more vociferous half were unable to understand. I thought that it was not worth the trouble to be involved in lengthy arguments with them and left the decision to future generations. I had no wish to be 'the grandest tiger in the jungle', as Little Black Sambo would have put it. However, this find started me off on a quest for information about the ancient gods of Britain which involved me in many avenues of research which I had never thought to explore. I published the results in a couple of popular books, *Gogmagog* and *Witches*, as well as in technical reports and thought that I had finished with the subject; but it has been with me in one way and another for more than a dozen years. What were gods? And why apparently had the bulk of mankind always believed that there were such things?

Of course there are many thoughtful answers from those who have made a real study of it all and it is very rash of me to offer any new ideas. But I do not think that there has been anything which seems completely satisfactory. Totemism, anthropomorphism, ancestor worship and the rest sound very convincing, but before we go any further, let me quote three verses from the sixth chapter of Genesis and see whether anything we have heard of really provides an answer:

And it came to pass, when men began to multiply on the
face of the earth, and daughters were born unto them,
that the sons of God saw the daughters of men that they were
fair; and they took them wives of all which they chose.
(verses 1 and 2)

Then follows verse 3 which seems to have no connection with
the first two and after that verse 4 takes up the story again :

There were giants in the earth in those days; and also after
that, when the sons of God came unto the daughters of
men, and they bare children to them, the same became mighty
men which were of old, men of renown.

Now how does this piece of legend fit in with any known 'ism'?
It is not totemism, anthropomorphism or anything of that kind.
It is a definite statement of fact that a race known as the sons of
God intermarried with another known as the daughters of men.
But who were the sons of God? This problem has puzzled me for
years and I have met no one who can supply the answer.

There is the same kind of thing in Greek mythology where one
race is apparently actually described as Gods. They have unions
with mortal women and produce heroes. One finds it, too, in the
northern lands. Many of our early Anglo-Saxon kings claimed to
be descended from Woden, that same Odin of the Norsemen, who
was the equivalent of the Greek Zeus, the chief of the gods.
Let us forget such terms as polytheism and see whether there is
any other explanation which might fit this seemingly impossible
situation. After all there are many people who believe that every
word in the Bible is true and to them the sons of God must mean,
not only that God had children, but that He also had a wife.

When I first thought about this matter, it seemed obvious that
the sons of God must have been some conquering race who
thought a lot of themselves and to whom it was at first unthinkable that they should actually intermarry with the people they
conquered. The whole caste system of India was apparently based
on such a situation. The race, formerly known as the Aryans and
now generally spoken of as Indo-Europeans, thought it sinful to
mix their blood with that of the people they had vanquished. But
they had gods of their own, not one. If they had been or believed
themselves to be of divine descent, they would have surely been

2

called the 'children of the gods'. Aryan appears to mean 'noble' and nothing more.

This problem is not entirely foreign to us in England. Very large numbers of people are known to have descended from Edward III. Edward III was descended in blood from Alfred. Alfred claimed descent from Woden. Are all these people then entitled to put 'son of God' after their name? Of course it sounds ridiculous when said like that but, funny or not, it is interesting to wonder whether they might be. Who was Woden anyway? Was he just the wandering chieftain of a barbarous war band, or was he something else?

So much difficulty lies in the meaning of words. A god to ancient Romans could be simply an outstanding man and he could be deified in his lifetime. We all know the unpleasant results of this process when Herod was hailed as a god by the populace! The practice of calling Roman emperors gods is also well known. It may appear strange to those who hold that the term only refers to the creator of the universe, but as a matter of historical fact it needs to be considered.

It is even more strange to find that the term 'devil' is simply a distortion of a word meaning 'god'. The gods of one religious belief became the devils of another. Lucifer, the light bearer, a god to many races (including the Celts, who called him Lugh), was also the wicked angel who was thrown out of heaven. Perhaps it is even more peculiar to learn that the original holder of the Greek title was the planet Venus and so female. Lucifer, Satan, the Devil, the dragon and the serpent all came to mean the spirit of evil, not only in the Christian world but in many others also, which brings us to a second curious puzzle: what was the war in heaven?

Unless the meaning is very obscure, I far prefer the language of the old James I Bible to that of the modern 'told to the children' versions and I think that there is nothing obscure in the following quotations which all bear on the same subject. The first is from Revelation, chapter 12, verses 7 to 9 and is the most complete statement of what was evidently, at the time of Nero, a very ancient legend:

And there was war in heaven: Michael and his angels
fought against the dragon; and the dragon fought and his

angels, and prevailed not; neither was their place found any more in heaven. And the great dragon was cast out, that old serpent, called the Devil, and Satan, which deceiveth the whole world : he was cast into the earth, and his angels were cast out with him.

Also in St Luke, chapter 10, verse 18, Jesus himself is reported as quoting : 'I beheld Satan as lightning fall from heaven.' These are not unique survivals in old Hebrew writings, for something similar is preserved by the Hindus, while the serpent or dragon is even found in old Norse mythology. There was a story spread widely in the ancient world that there had been a war in heaven and the vanquished side had been driven to live on earth.

Of course it is possible to reject anything of this sort as pure imagination by men long ago seeking for an explanation of the reason for the conflict between good and evil. In almost every ancient religion of which we have record there is this story of conflict between the powers of light and darkness. The ancient Greeks did not have it, but then their gods were quite frankly 'not respectable' in a Christian sense; neither were those of the Romans, Saxons, Norsemen or Celts. These had all the vices as well as many of the virtues of mankind. They were simply men and women with greatly enlarged powers.

If we take the view that all legends of this kind are no more than fiction, there is no point in going on with this study; but, as the years go by, it becomes increasingly clear that many, if not all, have some foundation in fact. They may be greatly embroidered and appear as fairy stories, but there is something in them based on memories of events which really happened. They are not the same as myths, which are the counterparts of religious ritual; although these themselves often contain genuine pieces of tradition. The long labours of Sir James Frazer which resulted in that ponderous series of books known as *The Golden Bough* brought this home to many readers. Tradition itself tells that he was locked up in his study for many hours a day by his ferocious French wife to compel him to write his daily quota. Certainly he seemed to wear a haunted look.

I am going to take it for granted that there was some truth at the back of the two scraps of legend which I have quoted and see whether we can find anything to suggest an explanation. It is a kind of exercise in detection, but it is not fiction. The guesses may be wrong, yet there is something to be investigated.

Our questions then are: who were the sons of God? and what was the war in heaven?

If anybody reads the early chapters of Genesis with care, it becomes clear that some editor has linked together at least two traditional accounts of the Creation with remarkably little skill. The Adam and Eve story is the kind of thing you might find in the religious beliefs of many an African tribe today and we need not bother with it yet. However the other, which in itself looks like a blend of more than one tale, has a lot of legend in it. At the very start of this we meet another puzzle in chapter 1, verse 26: 'And God said, Let us make man in our image, after our likeness.' Who did God say this to? We have always been led to understand that there was only one God and that He was absolute. He created everything from millions of nebulae to bacteria. Yet in the chief religious book of the early Hebrews He is pictured as talking to others of like form. Were they perhaps the sons of God? One can hardly assume that He was talking to Himself. It is even more remarkable when we find a similar kind of story preserved on the other side of the Atlantic. There several descendants of God are reported as having more than one trial at making man like themselves. There were also failures of the same kind as is described in Genesis. This is some world wide traditional story and not confined to the Hebrews. It seems most unlikely that it is more than some ancient theory, but at the same time we must observe that it had once a very wide distribution. How was it spread from one continent to another before the days of efficient ships?

Curiously enough this question is not confined to traditions. When I used to study archaeological problems in the Cambridge Museum of Archaeology and Ethnology, I happened to notice a similarity between some groups of ancient objects found on the two continents. Types of stone axes and little female figurines were strangely alike on both sides of the Atlantic. But, oddly enough, the two areas in which they had been found were not those closest together in distance. In fact they were the eastern shores of the Mediterranean and the islands of the Caribbean. At the time I took this similarity to be entirely accidental. In any case they were not large or important things with intricate patterns or anything of that sort. Still the resemblance could be observed and had it been noticed in, say, Norway and Denmark, would have been taken without demur as an indication of a former close connection between the two countries.

Of course many people have noted that pyramids were built both in ancient Central America and in Egypt and I well remember the violence of the academic quarrel when it was suggested that certain American carvings represented elephants. Perhaps they did. I was not impressed one way or the other, but I was greatly entertained by the rudeness of the old professors to their opponents. They are less outspoken today than they were at the end of the Kaiser's War.

All this was part of the great controversy which was known as 'diffusion versus independent invention'. One school of thought held that once something was invented the idea spread from one centre around the world—it was diffused. The other side believed that mankind frequently invented the same thing in different places. As an example of the kind of problem which could be raised, there is the comparatively recent case of the Jericho skulls. During the excavations in prehistoric Jericho, a collection of several human skulls was found. These had had clay faces modelled on the bones and cowrie shells set in the eye sockets. Precisely the same procedure was followed in New Guinea till quite lately. We had several modern examples in the Cambridge Museum. Both peoples were living in a Stone Age civilization, but separated in time by several thousand years. Had the people of New Guinea invented this curious custom on their own, or was it one which spread across land and sea and had endured for a vast period of time? It is such a curious custom that one would think that the answer in this case is diffusion. This would have caused great excitement two generations ago, but scarcely raised a ripple on the pool of anthropological thought today. Both archaeology and anthropology have become so specialized that few men or women remain who are capable of letting their minds range widely about the world.

To balance the scales between diffusion and independent invention, I had better mention another case. About fifteen years ago extensive settlements and burials of an early Eskimo community were found and excavated not far from Point Barrow in Alaska. At the time they were thought to be the earliest Eskimo

6

remains to have been discovered. When the published report reached me I was greatly astonished. It was evident that, although these arctic hunters were making the most delicate and beautiful flint implements, even finer and more competent than those of the famous 'laurel leaves' from the French palaeolithic cave of Solutré, yet they clearly showed by their carvings in ivory that they had once been well acquainted with the use of metal. There were long carved chains of interlocking rings. There were swivels obviously copied from iron ones and so on. Finally there were a very few tiny tools, one of which still had a minute iron blade in it. These men, although they had once been efficient users of metal tools, had been forced to become high artists in working flint which is always thought of as being a far more primitive condition. Their progress had not been evolution but devolution. They had, for some unknown reason, been compelled to adopt a more primitive way of life and their flint work was so similar to that of some of the Upper Palaeolithic perhaps 10,000 years earlier, that anyone might have been excused for thinking that the two cultures must have been closely related. This can surely have only been a case of independent invention.

Therefore it is quite unsafe to make comparisons between pyramids in Egypt and America with a view to saying that they had a common source. A pyramid after all is surely no more than a respectably constructed heap of stones : a burial cairn perhaps, modernized by a more civilized community.

However, our Eskimoes draw attention to another feature of the ancient world. Driven out from some unknown homeland over Bering Strait into a new continent, thrust into an arctic climate and eventually forced to adapt their square wooden houses to small stone hovels more suited to the cold, they had lost at the same time a vital source of supply. Iron was no longer obtainable. They must have looked back with sorrow to an age of iron where everything was much happier and easier. This is what we gather was the outlook of the ancient world on our side of the western ocean : they looked back to an 'age of gold' and not forward to one in the future. This seems very remarkable when we know how much thought their brilliant men expended on trying to explain the mysteries of the universe.

However, it is a well known trait of humanity to think that everything in the past was better than it is today. The old men

7

in sailing ships always looked back to the ship before their last one as the finest vessel that there ever was. They cursed the one they had just left as an unhandy hard-working bitch. But the one before that was an able beauty.

Archaeology on the other hand appears to tell of a progress, interrupted at times of course, from barbarous stone age to rocket propulsion and journeys to the planets. Why then the ancient belief in a past golden age? Was there ever such a period? You would have thought that men in an age when bronze tools were plentiful would have thought that their conditions had advanced enormously from those of their grandfathers. When iron became common, surely this was another great step forward. But suppose for a moment that there were such people on earth as the sons of God. Would they not presumably once have been as far ahead of the men of the iron age as those were ahead of the cave men of the palaeolithic? Their remote descendants born by the daughters of men might well have looked back to the golden age of their ancestors. So many legends, too, affirm that such and such a god taught mankind such and such an art. Hu the Mighty, for instance, so the Welsh Barddas say, taught men agriculture. Man did not evolve it himself by painfully scratching with a pointed stick in the ground : a god taught it to him. It is not so easy to say this story is just a piece of traditional imagination when all over the world you find primitive tales of gods teaching men essential techniques. There is a puzzle here which is not just a bee in my bonnet.

One of the most remarkable of all British legends does not directly concern gods, but is a warning to all who dismiss legend as without foundation. Ever since people started to take an interest in archaeology, Stonehenge has been one of the greatest sources of speculation. What was it for, when was it built and who built it? Many people have favoured an astronomical reason for its construction. This idea flourished for a while, was frowned upon and has recently been brought forward again. It was suggested that it was a kind of instrument for calculating the approach of eclipses, a sort of prehistoric observatory in fact. Callanish in the Outer Hebrides is put forward as another. But these monuments were apparently put up about four thousand years ago, or so it is generally thought today.

Stonehenge was undoubtedly set up at two different periods,

8

Figure 1 A. Rough sketch of Callanish avenues and circle from the south-east. Central pillar 15 feet high, mound of burial cairn to its right.
B. Rough plan of the monument. Overall length about 123 yards (*c*. 92 metres).

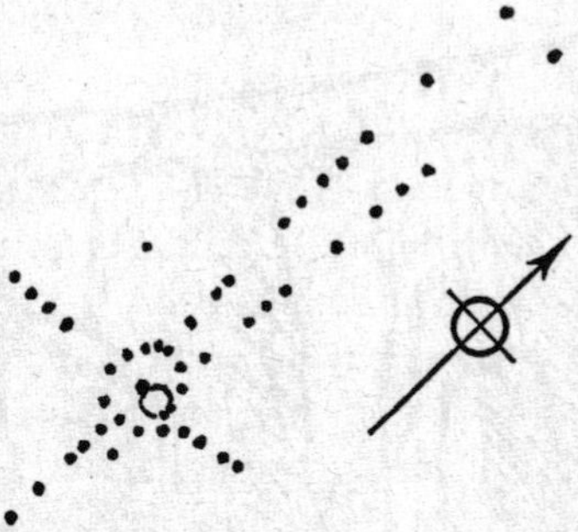

with two main and different types of stone. These are the trilithons, like stone goal posts, and they are made of a local stone known as Sarsen from the Marlborough downs. They were dressed with mauls and constructed with considerable skill. The other stones are not local. They were imported from a very long distance away and most are described geologically as 'spotted diorites'. The nearest place where such rock was easily obtained was Prescelly Top in the south-west corner of Wales. Archaeology assumes that, however it was done, they were brought from there.

Now in the reign of Henry I a cleric known as Geoffrey of Monmouth wrote a *British history*, using, as he claimed, an older book which he had found. Much of what he wrote is now thought to have been faked; however, even if this is so, how did he know as much as he evidently did about Stonehenge which he calls 'the Giants' Dance'. The thing had been set up perhaps three thousand years before he wrote his history.

The story he tells is this: some time in the later fifth century after Christ, the British leader, Aurelius, worsted the Saxon invaders and wished to put up a monument to the memory of his compatriots who had been murdered at a conference. The magician, Merlin, was consulted. He said that the proper thing to do was to fetch the magic circle, the Giants' Dance, from Ireland. Its stones promoted healing. The stones were to be found

Figure 2 Rough sketch of part of the circle at Stonehenge. The bluestones are in front and the Sarsen trilithons behind. These are not the huge trilithon arches, but the sketch shows how relatively small the bluestones are.

on a mountain called Killaraus. Unwillingly Aurelius's Britons, under Uther Pendragon, invaded Ireland, defeated the Irish and brought back the Giants' Dance.

Now it is extremely uncertain whether Aurelius ever existed and apparently quite impossible that he imported the Dance. Yet Geoffrey knew that it was imported. Even more interesting than this, there are diorites in Ireland, fifteen miles north of Dublin, as well as further north and west. Was Geoffrey more correct than modern archaeologists and if so how did he get his knowledge? It is difficult to see what answer there can be to this, yet there must be one. This tale is surely quite one of the most remarkable in all ancient history. A cleric writing in Oxford, in the days when men believed that the sun went round a flat earth, knew that the bluestones, the diorites, had been brought to Stonehenge from over the sea and also indicated a land of origin where such stones are found today. It took men with microscopes to learn such things again.

There is even more in Geoffrey's legend than this, for he makes Merlin say that the stones were connected with giants in the farthest coast of Africa. Only in 1953 was it appreciated that a carving of a dagger on a Sarsen at Stonehenge was perhaps a representation of such things used in Mycenaean Greece about 1600 B.C. Africa was not far out. Several carvings of axes on the same stone resembled those common in Britain and Ireland also in the Early Bronze Age.

Now it is clear that Geoffrey's *History* is a mixture of fairy tale and legend, with facts dotted about here and there in the wrong places. Still a legend is a legend even if it has been used to illustrate a fictitious interpretation of history. Geoffrey must have heard a tale about the Giants' Dance which was genuine legend. How otherwise could he have thought that the stones had been brought from overseas?

It is, I think, of general interest to take this problem further and see what we can learn from it. As I frequently say in reports and books, I do not expect to get the answers right, but it is better to try than to sit down and swallow blindly everything that is told us by people who may know even less than we do.

Now supposing that some Norman monk or knight, who had been campaigning in Ireland, had brought back a genuine tradition and this had got into some old manuscript which Geoffrey had seen, then probably Geoffrey had written down the name of the place where the stones had actually come from. He called it Killaraus and evidently thought that people would know where this was. The only attempt to identify it I happen to have seen or heard of is by another medieval writer, Giraldus Cambrensis who amongst other things wrote a *Topography of Ireland* in about A.D. 1186. Geoffrey's *History* was written about forty years before this. Both men were ecclesiastics of high standing and had either been bishops or deputized for bishops. As learning went in those days, they ranked very high.

Giraldus copied a précis of Geoffrey's legend into his *Topography*, but, apparently mistaking an 'a' for a 'd', he said the stones were brought from Kildare near the castle of Naas and that some stones still stood there.

Now Killaraus is the earlier form of the name and I do not see why we should neglect it. I will make my own attempt at identification, but do not necessarily believe me. I know a little Gaelic, or Erse as it used to be called.

Geoffrey was writing in Latin. Therefore he put a Latin sounding '—us' on the end of his place name. Killaraus was something like Killaradh, or Killary. The 'Kill' part of the word is a Christian Erse word meaning a cell or church. There are hundreds of them in Ireland and Scotland. 'Ary', however, is probably a river name like the 'aray' in Inveraray in Argyll. Killaraus is therefore 'the church on the Ary'. If Geoffrey's legend had any truth in it, the church should be somewhere not far from an area where the spotted diorites could be found and such rocks are probably still there today. One of these areas, according to the geological maps, is not far to the west of Tipperary. Everyone has heard of Tipperary, but probably has not noticed that it is on a river Ary.

Tipperary is an anglicized Erse name. The modern Irish map makers have spelt it Tiobaid arann. We should probably spell it 'Tobar' and 'ary' meaning the spring, or well, on the ary, just as Tobermory in Mull is Tobar Mahri, Mary's well. This may be a simple coincidence and there may be several claimants for Geoffrey's Killaraus, but it is certainly significant that there is this river Ary within reasonable distance of a patch of diorites. Moreover the Ary, after a few miles, joins the big river Suir which meets the sea at Waterford. The significance of this will appear as we go on. In any case Killaraus is not a Welsh name but an Erse one and you could not find it near Prescelly in Wales.

However, there is another coincidence which needs some consideration. During the Second World War the Admiralties of several countries made use of an unorthodox method of tracking hostile vessels. A form of dowsing was employed in which a pendulum was used over a chart to follow the course of the enemy ship or submarine. This appears to have been quite successful. Although this magic seems quite impossible to most people, I have been experimenting with it for many years now and see that it does in fact give apparently reliable results. I do not really believe it, yet it works and one must give it some attention. A variant of the method can also be used to find the dates of objects which can be checked to some extent by testing the ages of people from their handwriting.

Wishing to see whether I could learn anything from the actual bluestones of Stonehenge themselves, I asked R. S. Newall, who had done much archaeological work there, whether he had any small chips from them. He very kindly sent me six little fragments which I then tested.

The first point to be examined was the actual date of the setting up of the circle at Stonehenge itself and to this the pendulum gave the answer of 1870 B.C. to the nearest ten years. The actual official date at present, which is probably little more than a guess, is 1650–1500 B.C. Since one can see no reason why the pendulum should give any sensible answer at all, this seems remarkable.

The next experiment was to try to find from a map where the pendulum thought the stones came from. I say pendulum, but of course this is only an indicator. The actual process must be in the operator's mind. I have discussed this at length in several books and need not do so here.

The method I used, which probably differs from those employed in hunting submarines and such like activities, was this. I set a map of the British Isles north and south. On it I put a chip from a bluestone. Between myself and the chip of stone I swung a pendulum on a few inches of cord gently to and fro. With the other hand I moved a wooden pointer slowly over the map. For most of the time the pendulum oscillated, went backwards and forwards, monotonously. However, when the pointer was over Stonehenge the pendulum went into a circular swing. The bluestones are still there and it said so. From Prescelly, however, there was no reaction. There are bluestones, diorites, there we know, but they were not the right ones. I moved on to Ireland.

Now if you are looking for the shortest sea route, the diorite beds a few miles north of Dublin are the obvious choice but nothing happened. Neither did the pendulum fancy any of the beds in northern Ireland. In Tipperary it was another story. Not only did the pendulum circle, gyrate, over the beds to the westward of the town, it also did so near the place itself.

I tried this place on the map for the date of the setting up of the original circle of bluestones and got an answer of 2650 B.C., a great deal earlier than any modern reckoning for Stonehenge. As I have said before, I do not really believe this, but I have tried other ancient monuments. The Merry Maidens and the Pipers near Lamorna in Cornwall gave the dates 2540 and 2610 B.C. I don't think anyone has any idea of what their real dates might be.

The Merry Maidens circle, unlike most megaliths, seems to be complete. There is a ring of squared granite blocks standing upright on a little hill top, with an entrance to the east and pointers to the west. On a fine day I went up to the circle, set the pendulum at thirty inches, which is the rate for age, put my hand on top of a stone and set the thing swinging. I agreed mentally to count ten years for each turn the instrument made. I have already said the computation must be somehow in the operator's mind.

Figure 3 Rough sketch of the Merry Maidens near Lamorna, Cornwall, looking north-east. The average stone is about 4 feet high. Pendulum date *c*. 2540 B.C.

As soon as the pendulum started to swing, a strange thing happened. The hand resting on the stone received a strong tingling sensation like a mild electric shock and the pendulum itself shot out until it was circling nearly horizontally to the ground. The stone itself, which must have weighed over a ton, felt as if it were rocking and almost dancing about. This was quite alarming, but I stuck to my counting. At 451 turns the gyration stopped and the ball returned to its back and forth swing. I was counting in tens, which made the real number 4510 and subtracting the present year from this you get an approximate date of 2540 B.C. to the nearest ten years. The next day I sent my wife up alone to see what happened to her. She had the same experience. It has happened nowhere else. The Pipers were mute and so were many crosses and other monuments which I tried. But most circular monuments are now incomplete and perhaps something has gone from them.

The reader is perfectly at liberty to believe that my wife and I imagined all this, but, if so, there is no point in their reading this book. It is for people with wider knowledge of what anthropologists call 'the odd' and this is found in all groups of humanity everywhere in the world. It ranges from 'couvade', where the father of an unborn child feels ill before its birth, to the 'pointing bone' of the witch doctor who by this kills his enemy. Those who have had any dealings with the odd are not interested in the disbelief of those who have not. Actually research with the pendulum shows that many who cannot, or will not, appreciate the odd frequently have something lacking in their nervous system. Their bodily bio-electronic potential is too low and they are actually incapable of experiencing it. It is similar to being colourblind or tone-deaf. Colour-blindness effects about one male in ten; odd-blindness about one in three. Perhaps therefore one person in three can never see a ghost, experience telepathy or work a pendulum or divining rod. For some reason this often turns them to frantic denial of the existence of the faculty. It is probably subconscious irritation at not being completely human!

However, we will leave a discussion of the Merry Maidens for the present and return to the Giants' Dance. We will not even discuss the apparent difficulty in transporting the stones from one country to another for the moment. We will go back to an unexpected statement in Geoffrey of Monmouth's story, the question of the Giants at the far end of the Mediterranean. This brings us back to the original Bible statement that the offspring of the sons of God were giants.

Now the old Irish chronicles spoke of a race of warlike merchants and sailors who came to Ireland and held parts of it under tribute. They were known as the Fomor, men from below the ocean's rim. At first they were clearly men but today, and by Geoffrey's time, fomor has come to mean a giant. Sometimes they had several rows of teeth. They vanished from history, but apparently not from the world. Several surnames today are probably fomorian in origin : Morgan Macnamarra and Morrison, all meaning 'son of the sea', and Murdoch meaning seaman. Captain Thomas, who charted the seas of the west of Scotland, observed this long ago as evidence for a lost tribe of sons of the sea. Most of the other Highland tribes were men of the Cat, Bull, Stag, Boar and other totems. Of course all this is very nebulous and shunned like the plague by respectable archaeologists who prefer to leave legend and folk-lore severely alone. But it interests me because my mother's maiden name was actually Murdoch and her father claimed to be their chief, although they are now a sept of the MacDonalds. In Wales, Scotland and Ireland then you still find men whose ancestors long, long ago seem to have come from some unknown land beyond the ocean. They were not the Irish tribes who the chroniclers said had Greek in their ancestry, but something else. One cannot help wondering whether Geoffrey was right and they were perhaps Minoans from Crete. But, if they were, there is a history of navigation here in primitive ships, which is quite as remarkable as any in maritime adventure. The men who set up the standing stone circles and alignments of stones passed by sea right up the western coasts of Britain and Ireland. Their monuments still stand in the Outer Hebrides and in the Northern Isles. They were indeed the sons of the sea and, if you are to cross the Minch, or navigate through the Pentland Firth, no one is going to persuade me that it was frequently done in a dugout canoe. I know these waters. Having been on the bridge of a vessel in summer, which stood on end in the Pentland Firth till one appeared to be looking at the bottom of the ocean, it would take a lot to make me believe that men often crossed it in dugout canoes to set up the standing stones of Stennis. But that is all that archaeologists appear to know. Dugout canoes have been found in the silts of the Clyde. They are concrete evidence of early man; but there were other vessels of which no trace is likely to be preserved and in these men could travel safely over miles of a waste of seas. We know that they existed in the northern Bronze Age, because pictures of them are engraved on the rocks of Norway. They were built of wooden

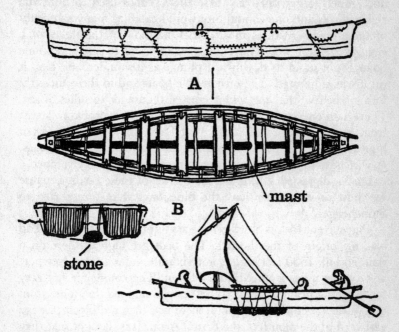

Figure 4 A. Small West Greenland umiak which I measured in 1937.
B. Suggested method of transporting stones, slung between a pair of skin boats. Owing to rawhide lashings there would be little chafing.

frames and covered with sewn skins. Caesar learnt the way to build them in Britain and had some constructed himself to ferry men across rivers in his civil war in Spain. Here and there they survived into my lifetime at any rate. I have been out in an Irish curragh and measured an Eskimo umiak. The cobles of North-umberland are wooden descendants of skin boats for their name is derived from the Welsh ceuobol, which means just that. While another descendant is the Saveiro seine boat of Portugal, pulled by four great oars, which is just a flat bottomed skin boat now built of wood.

Let us look at the Eskimo umiak for a moment, for its construction is just the same as those on the Norwegian rock engravings published by Guttorm Gjessing. The one I measured was only twenty-four feet long, but it is known that there were once much larger ones. In these the Eskimos used to hunt the right whales and one community would catch as many as twenty of these great creatures in a year. One blow of the flukes of a right whale's tail would have smashed an umiak to pieces, yet these boats could stand its downward plunge as it sounded and play it till it was exhausted. These were able boats and in their ancestral forms I believe that the fomor crossed thousands of miles of sea. There was one other trick that the Eskimo had probably learnt from the navigators of antiquity. They knew how to fasten buoyancy floats of blown-up skin to the gunwales of their vessels. It was next to impossible to overturn a skin boat so equipped.

I have digressed a little on the matter of these boats, because we must now consider how the bluestones were transported to Stonehenge.

The current idea is based on the assumption that Prescelly Top was the origin of the diorites. The beds are high up here on a pointed hill, 1500 feet high, some six miles inland from Newport and twelve miles from Milford Haven. The country is not easy for dragging heavy weights. Whether you shipped the stones from one or the other of these places, there was then a difficult passage eastward to the mouth of the Bristol Avon. It is thought that they were rafted along this coast. I don't know whether any of the believers in this theory have any experience of rafts in the sea, but I can assure them that it is not the fun that anyone might think. I have tried it long ago off the coast of north Devon near the Foreland and I did not like it at all. Unless a raft is very big, it is surprisingly cranky. Certainly the reconstruction in the official guide to Stonehenge is completely impossible.

Even supposing you have managed to navigate your raft round from Pembrokeshire, past where Cardiff now stands, there must have been a new hazard. There is more water in the sea today than there was in the early Bronze Age. You can tell this because various early structures and fresh water peat beds are now beneath the sea at high tide. It therefore seems clear that the banks and bars at the mouth of the Severn would have extended much further west than they do today, making the mouth of the Bristol Avon far more difficult to enter. Approaching this lee shore with unhandy rafts could have been a desperate undertaking. In fact I hardly think that anyone would have attempted it at the end of a long passage on a raft from the west.

Still, let us suppose that you have got into the mouth of the Bristol Avon and paddled your raft up it as far as it will go, there still remains a very long portage before you. Somehow you have to transport a stone weighing a ton and a half up hill and down dale for about six miles and then ship it again for a further river passage.

There is another point, too, which has to be considered: England was raw and new. Hills were covered in tangled woodland and valley bottoms with marshes. Of course, with a considerable labour force and unlimited time, it could be done. The stones could be hauled up hills when once a track had been cut and they could have been rolled on corduroy pathways over the bogs. Give me a sea passage every time.

However, if Geoffrey of Monmouth was right and the stones did in reality come from Ireland, if the pendulum is right and they did come from somewhere near Tipperary, the task was by no means so difficult. Tipperary is handy to a big river, the Suir. From the mouth of the Suir at Waterford, supposing you have reasonable sea transport, it is a straight 140 miles deep water passage to Land's End. You are not running on to a lee shore all the time, as you would be from Prescelly to the Bristol Avon. From there it is the course, once well known to most Englishmen in the old song 'Spanish Ladies':

'The first land we saw was the point called the Dodman,
Thence Rame Head in Plymouth, Start, Portland and Wight.'

and so on up the channel to Christchurch and the mouth of the other Avon. Once up that past Salisbury to West Amesbury it is only a mile and a half haul up and on to the downs to Stonehenge itself. The sea route is shorter than the one taken by many small yachts every year in the Fastnet race.

Could such a voyage be made by sea nearly four thousand years ago? Of course it could, if you get dugouts and rafts out of your head. As recently as the period between the two Great

Figure 5 Sketchmap showing places mentioned in the text in connection with the problem of the old stone monuments.

Wars, if two big warships had to pass in a narrow channel, such as the Suez Canal, they had to be warped out of each other's way. That means that an anchor, known as a kedge, had to be laid out ahead and to one side of each vessel. When it was secure on the bottom, each vessel was hauled towards it by main force and the two ships passed each other crabwise. Now these kedge anchors were of great weight, far more than a bluestone, and behind them trailed a length of huge steel cable. No boat could carry such a weight at its stern, for it would be pulled under. But two thirty-foot boats carried it easily, slung between them in the water. They formed a kind of catamaran, a single vessel with two hulls. In the water, as everybody knows, the anchor is of much less weight.

Whether this is still done today I do not know, but it was a practice going far back into the days of sail and was probably known in high antiquity. Now surely we can see how the bluestones were transported. You took two large skin boats, buoyant as corks, and lashed a platform of spars across their gunwales. Beneath this, and in the water, the bluestone was slung in rawhide ropes. You took it down the river Suir and then you sailed it, with an umiak's square sail in the fore part of each boat, straight across to Land's End and so on up the channel. With reasonable westerly summer wind the first leg may have taken no more than two days. A week could have seen it at Christchurch.

Geoffrey pictures Ambrosius as ridiculing the idea that it was possible and Merlin as solving the problem. Was Merlin perhaps some earlier Archimedes? What is magic in one age is the commonplace of the next.

It is interesting to see, too, that the stones were believed to possess great healing properties. Water was poured over them and sick persons bathed in it. This practice survived in the highlands of Scotland into recent times. Such famous charm stones as the Clach dearg were dipped into water which sick cattle were made to drink. Diorites are volcanic rocks and not very different from granites. Some granites are radio-active and thought by a few authorities to be a cause of cancer. There may have been some unknown healing properties in the diorites, unlikely though it may seem.

However the people who brought the stones across the sea can hardly have been the fomor, unless of course they were another branch of the same people. This may well be. The archaeological picture seems to suggest that for much of the Bronze Age one culture covered the whole of the south and east of Britain and that it had close connections with Ireland. Axes of bronze apparently cast in Ireland were distributed all over the area, as well as spears and other metal objects. Irish bronzes in fact have been found as far away as the bottom of Cadiz harbour. An obvious link exists, too, between the middle Bronze Age culture in the south of Britain and that of the eastern end of the Mediterranean. There is also reasonable evidence that the Bronze Age civilization of southern England can only have been under the control of a single power centred near Stonehenge. So little, however, is really known, although a great deal is talked, that all this must at present remain hypothetical. Be this as it may, some central control was obviously responsible for ordering and carrying out the transport of the stones, whether from Wales or Ireland. The picture of shaggy, deformed men given in the official handbook could be very far from the truth. 'There were giants . . . in those days', if not in stature, at least in mentality. Except, as suggested by Geoffrey, in Ireland, there can have been no opposition to the removal of the Giants' Dance. Someone said 'Let this be done' and it was done. The picture of numerous little chieftains dotted here and there about the country, as there evidently were in the succeeding Iron Age, does not hold good for the earlier Bronze Age. Warlike men no doubt there were, for bronze spears are very common; yet some overriding authority is implied, not only by the widespread similarity of the objects discovered, but by the transport of the stones themselves.

Towards the end of the Bronze Age the climate is known to have become very much worse and wetter. Great peat beds formed in the west. Tribes moved about all over the western world looking for new land. England was invaded by frequent Celtic settlers. The descendants of the Bronze Age population may well have looked back to a former golden age : a time of settled rule, when merchants could bring them goods from all over the known world without too much danger from weather or from local strife.

Before we leave Stonehenge, there is another problem of general interest. Although the Sarsen stones, the local sandstones which were built as arches, do not present a transport problem as much as the bluestones, the manner in which they were set up has always been a puzzle. No traces of earthen ramps up which the lintels could have been hauled have ever been found in excavations. Some other method was employed. There is not so much difficulty about setting up the great doorposts. I have seen in 1921 a 200 foot mast made of bolted tree trunks set on end in Jan Mayen by the simple expedient of dropping another tree, attached to the head of the mast, away from it. The upright stones could have been raised in this manner. The difficulty comes when the lintel has to be put on top of the upright.

The present idea is that they were raised foot by foot on a glorified woodpile made of tree trunks. But anyone who has worked on top of a woodpile knows how much logs roll. It would have taken a very great deal of lashing to keep the thing moderately steady. I could not think how it was done, till I got

Figure 6 Rough sketches of two crude Christian wheel-headed crosses set up on the road passing the Merry Maidens, presumably in a vain attempt to destroy their influence. The cross on the short stone might suggest an archaeological dating of about A.D. 750 but the pendulum gives *c*. A.D. 910-920 for both. Both cross-heads are 2 feet in diameter.

a telephone call last Christmas Eve from Monica English, the artist. 'I know how they did it,' she said. 'Did what?' I asked expectantly. 'Put up those stones,' she said as if I was half-witted not to know at once. 'They did it in the snow.' Then I saw it in a flash. There were ice tracks of hard packed snow along which the stone monsters could be hauled with comparative ease. There was no need for a mass of rollers, for the block would slide. Then there were slippery ramps up which the lintels could be hauled and slid easily on to the tenons provided for them on the heads of the uprights. Then in the summer all the ice melted and the operation looked like magic. The mystery has remained all these centuries, but I think Monica has provided the answer, which has floored so many learned men. Six thousand pounds, I was told, it cost to replace one capstone a few years ago. In the Bronze Age the snow apparently did it for them. A whole great temple was put up, to be the wonder of the western world. Of course, that is, if there was enough snow for the purpose and if the frost lasted long enough. It does not do so today, but we are told that in the early part of the Bronze Age winters were colder and summers were hotter. In the later part there was much more precipitation than there is today. It looks as if the snow may have been easy to get and also I know from personal observation in excavating early Bronze Age barrows that sturdy ponies were available to pull the stones.

TWO

I may seem to have been wandering a long way from my first two questions, yet it is not really so. They are bound up somehow with the evidence for an extraordinary spread of people all up the western seaboard of Europe who put up very great numbers of large upright stones for some apparently inexplicable reason. Single ones are perhaps not of very great interest, for they might mark the site where someone had been killed, or be a boundary between two different communities. But when you find great rings and lines of stones set up in Brittany, Cornwall, Wiltshire, Ireland, the Outer Hebrides and the Orkneys, it surely means something of vast importance to the people who put them up. No one has the least idea why great rows of stones were set striding over Dartmoor, nor why a huge ring was erected at Stennis in Orkney. Only one thing is obvious and that is that a race of seamen must have done it for an important purpose. Why do seamen put up marks? As far as I know it is only for one purpose and that is to show themselves or other seafarers how to get to some place in safety. But many of these indicators are far inland and could not be seen from the sea at all. Although the suggestion may seem fantastic, could it possibly be that they were meant to be seen from the air?

No, I am not crazy, but, although I have had no personal experience of the matter, I cannot fail to be impressed by the bulk of testimony that unidentified flying vehicles are frequently observed in our skies. Could it be that, in the Bronze Age and before, they were also numerous and needed direction points?

Let us go back to the ancient Greek gods. Till the second half of this century, it would have been quite absurd to suggest that there might have been some truth in the flying chariots which the gods possessed and the thunderbolts which Zeus threw. Furthermore it would have been ridiculous to think that these gods might have come from an unknown part of the universe and sometimes begotten children on women of the earth. It is no longer absurd—clumsy though our efforts may appear to be, man is already starting on his first tentative exploration of other planets and is there any reason to be sure that he is the first race to do so? Obviously the answer is 'no'. We have really very little idea of what may go on in outer space and it is an impertinence to think that man on Earth is the most advanced of all creation.

The Greek gods passed with great rapidity from their home on Mount Olympus to anywhere they wanted to go and if they were said to go in flying chariots, this only described the fastest things that man had by that time invented. It was all rather fantastic and even a little comical, but why did men believe anything of the sort unless sometime, somewhere, something of a vague resemblance to this picture had once existed? It was not only the product of Greek imagination, for there were Hindu stories, too, of godlike personages who actually had remarkable flying machines and destructive weapons. Nobody knew how they worked, of course, and it was all long ago. So was the chariot of fire, which took Elijah up into the heavens. I do not believe all this, of course, for there is very little to go on; but I do think that there is enough to make us wonder whether there is a possibility that for a short period long ago there may have been visitors to this earth from another and that they were so relatively advanced in technology as to be completely bewildering to the earth men of those days. If there were visitors of this kind, it is more than likely that they would need landing signs here and there. Supposing that they were beginning to investigate an unexplored world, which was completely unmapped and they were putting down a few parties of explorers, it would be necessary to have indications where these parties had been dropped. What would be more natural than to enlist native help to set up such marks?

It is hard for us today to visualize the Britain of, for instance, five thousand years ago. The vast extent of natural woodland is unknown today, except in tropical vegetation. Brambles and fallen trees made paths through it extremely difficult and it covered the bulk of the country. Only on some downlands was passage relatively easy and that was not free from large patches of juniper trees, thorn bushes, gorse and bramble. The wide vistas of rolling grassland did not exist. One can assume that exploration parties would be dropped on the edges of all this and traces of them would be found, if at all, in the kind of situations where we do find these stone set rings and alignments today. A stone ring would be noticeable from the air, just because such things do not often happen in nature. Neither would straight lines be frequent.

But there may have been another reason for setting up the stones, even if its object was the same. For untold generations it has been believed, especially by the devotees of the old witch religion, that by means of exciting people to execute wild circular dances, power could be generated and stored in stones or trees. Actually this appears to be scientific fact. It has been demonstrated by Mr P. Callagan in America that moths generate bio-electricity by the heat caused by the movements of their wings and they use this to locate their mates or food supply. I have described how I detected the same thing with beetles in *The Monkey's Tail*. This is observed fact and no longer something on the fringe of knowledge. Now if you have a large number of excited people dancing wildly round in a ring, you obviously generate a great deal of this bio-electricity, living electricity. If you carry out this performance in rings formed of stones with gaps between them, you have a form of dynamo. It has been shown that the electro-magnetic fields of stones, trees and water will absorb bio-electricity from outside and this is the probable reason why some people see ghosts in situations which were favourable to such impressions being preserved. I have elsewhere suggested the names of oread fields for those of stones, dryad fields for those of trees and naiad fields for those of streams in accordance with the Greek belief that nymphs with these names were to be found in such places.

We now apparently see why my wife and I experienced electric shocks when trying to date the stones of the circle of the Merry Maidens in Cornwall. The bio-electronic force had been stored at one time by the exertion of dancers in that circle and it had never been taken out again. The circle is still complete. But why did anybody wish to store up electronic power in such places? What possible use could it be put to?

Well, experiments with the pendulum have shown that the electronic fields about an object are double cones of limitless height and depth. It has also been shown that a pendulum length of the same radius as the base of the double cone will register contact with that cone. If, then, you had an apparatus in a flying machine set to the right wave length, you could pick up the rays from the stored energy in the stones and home on it like the moth to its mate. These rings of stones could have been used both as visible and invisible navigational beacons.

This suggestion sounds absurd to those who have got no further than believing that the stones were set up by shaggy and uncultured savages whose only aids to life were stone tools and soft, badly baked pottery. But what if there were two completely different races of people involved, the sons of God and the daughters of men?

Of course, I may well be talking complete rubbish, but before the reader dismisses it as such, perhaps he will tell me why the stones were set up at all. In the whole of western Europe, it used to be done and in the same area the excited ring dances were once commonplace. No one can give a reason for either. When explorers get up tributaries of the Amazon, they find the naked women of unknown tribes dancing in excited rings in forest glades. It is no answer to say that primitive man does this as a primitive religious rite and you did it in a sacred circle of stones or trees to make it more religious. Or children do it naturally and so it is a natural form of worship. But do any children do it unless they are first taught by some elder who has herself been taught as a child? What were the dances of Baal which so upset the Hebrew prophets? The Baalim were little stone jujus of the gods and the people danced before them to put power into the stones. The One God, Yahweh, was not supposed to like it. It was not only the Hebrew prophets who had this trouble. If you read the *Koran* of the Muslims, you find that Mahomet had the same difficulty with numerous godlings. We may think perhaps that these Baalim represented the sons of God, but with the passage of time nobody really remembered what that meant.

As a purely hypothetical exercise then, let us put up a probably absurd problem. Was there a long time ago, perhaps five thousand or more years it might have been, a series of exploratory visits to this world from another? Did they have considerable contact with the people then living on earth, including some degree of intermarriage? Did the explorers persuade the natives to help them in setting up direction beacons and similar constructions in return for being taught how to work metals, practise agriculture and even build primitive towns? Then, for some unknown reason, did it all come to an end, leaving some degree of hybrid population behind it? Were the visitors known as the sons of God, because they had a belief in a single deity?

I think it is impossible to imagine a large immigration of people from elsewhere. Had there been anything of the sort and had settlements been formed of foreigners, it seems impossible for no trace of them to have come to light. So much digging and construction work has been done that some totally unknown culture of objects must have emerged somewhere for the acute bewilderment of archaeologists. This has not happened. There are stories published of a very few unknown things being found in rocks, but until I see quite a numerous collection of such things I shall not believe it. Archaeological study is really quite advanced and I think we can say with confidence that no such foreign culture has yet come to light. You may say that Atlantis, Mu and even Tartessos have not yet been found and I say we have no vestige anywhere of any Atlantian culture, which must have existed, other than on the drowned lands, if there had been one. The Atlantis at present claimed at the eastern end of the Mediterranean cannot be right, because Atlantis was outside the Pillars of Hercules, that is west of Gibraltar. If it existed at all, one would have thought that the shoals off Cape Trafalgar might mark its grave. Yet the only unexpected things dredged from the bottom of nearby Cadiz harbour are Irish bronzes, and Irish goldwork has been found as far away as Palestine while Greek and Egyptian ornaments have been found in Bronze Age graves in Britain. People got about the world all right in those far off days, so where are the traces of the Atlantians who are said to have been so advanced that they had flying machines?

Perhaps, however, Atlantis was just another explorers' base and quite small. If so, there might be very little to find except the equivalent of the empty bully beef tins of the explorers of my day.

At least we buried these out of a sense of decency, now lacking in the bulk of our population, even in the wastes of Jan Mayen or Baffin Land.

This investigation becomes more and more complicated as it goes on. Nothing seems to have an obvious answer and yet all sorts of books are written and hundreds of lectures given about this very period, none of which give us much hint of the astonishing things which have taken place in a raw, new world some five thousand years ago.

The sea journey today from Kyle of Lochalsh opposite Skye on the Scottish mainland to Stornoway on Lewis in the Outer Hebrides is more than twice the distance from Dover to Calais and, even in summer, the passage is often cold, wet and stormy. Of course it is not so far from Duntulm in the north of Skye, out north past the Shiant Isles, but it is still twenty-five miles. Yet somewhere, perhaps five thousand years ago, men crossed in some numbers. About fourteen miles west of Stornoway, near the shores of Loch Roag, stands one of the most remarkable stone monuments in western Europe. And it is not the only one on that strange and desolate strip of country. Up to about a hundred years ago only the tops of the stones showed above a deep blanket of peat, which covered all that area. Now for several miles the peat has been removed and burnt. Beneath is the land surface on which the stones were put up and the land surface is under cultivation once again as it probably was before the wet period of the Later Bronze Age.

The standing stones of Callanish are in their way quite as remarkable as those of Stonehenge, for they form a strange pattern. In the middle is a single pillar fifteen feet high with a small and, probably later, rifled megalithic tomb at its foot. The central pillar forms the hub of a circle of stones enclosing an area thirty-seven feet across, of about the size of a tennis court. From this radiate one double and three single lines of uprights. They nearly form a cross, but do not quite do so. It is a strange and rather uncanny place to see in the usual pouring rain as it stands on a low hill. The double avenue heads almost true north for nearly a hundred yards.

Loch Roag is divided into two by the island of Bernera, which fits into it rather like a biscuit stuck in a dog's mouth. On the shore of Bernera facing Callanish are two more standing stones, looking as if they once marked a path across to the island where now is sea. It was probably dry land when the stones were put up, for fresh water Bronze Age peats can be seen round the shore today several feet below high tide mark.

Archaeologists as a whole pay little attention to Callanish. It does not appear strange to them that such a remarkable construction should be found in such a remote setting. If it had been found in Kent or Gloucestershire it would be thronged, but in the Outer Islands nobody cares. Yet it is the very situation of the thing which is so strange. It stands far out on the rim of the western ocean and there seems to be no possibility that there can ever have been a large population out there. Why should there be? The land must at the best of times have always been very poor. The Ring of Stennis in Orkney is not so strange, for the Orkneys are not so bleak as this stretch of the Long Island.

Not long ago it was suggested that Callanish was raised as a kind of substation of Stonehenge and both were intended as observatories to plot lunar eclipses. Even if this idea were correct, it implies a great organization far away who could journey to the distant north and either bring their labour with them or collect enough local men to do the work. I do not feel that it makes sense. Neither do I see how any great religious idea could have been called into play. Why put it there? There must have been more populous areas elsewhere, where such things could have been needed.

However, suppose that some survey party had been dropped out there to look for minerals or any other purpose, it might have been necessary to construct a landing mark of identifiable shape so that supplies could be dropped, or the explorers could be picked up when their time was up. Callanish in Lewis and Stennis in Orkney, could they not have been the identification signals set up by two exploration parties to draw attention to themselves, so that there would be no doubt where their bases were situated? All this would be hundreds of years before another station, the bluestone ring, was transported to Stonehenge.

If this possibly absurd suggestion has any foundation in fact, was it all in vain? Were none of these stations ever collected again because something happened to their home planet? Did these pioneers work their way back to more developed lands and there, by their superior technical knowledge, become for a time sons of

God? Did they naturally become kings and rulers and try to keep their stock reasonably distinct for thousands of years, until philosophers formulated the idea that all men were equal? Probably we will never know the answer, but it is possible to ask the question now; first because men are beginning to make exploratory expeditions to other worlds themselves and second because a very great quantity of information is being published suggesting that unknown flying machines may be coming from outside to examine our own planet. As I said before, I have had no experience of this, yet I find the mass of observed facts needs an explanation.

There seems to be a considerable difference between the monuments on the outlying islands and peninsulas and others far inland. They may represent successive stages in some form of exploratory development. If I am right in identifying Tipperary, its situation is not unlike that of Stonehenge, being convenient to river systems and old trackway routes along both of which native labour could be called in to help. Another famous circle, Avebury, could have been the original central point in the south of Britain before Stonehenge was thought of. If we are trying to plot the possible plan of exploration, then Avebury would come high on the list. But Avebury was less convenient by water though better situated for movements by land.

Of course the most dramatic of all these constructions in the west, for the later Stonehenge is in a different category, is Carnac on Quiberon Bay in Brittany. Here the remains of eleven long avenues of standing stones still survive, with parts of a great stone circle largely ruined by recent houses. The stone avenues apparently once extended for several miles and over a thousand stones still remain in place. If there was a central base where power was generated to operate bio-electronic beacons, this would have been the place. Although much further south, it stands in a somewhat similar position to Callanish, with a drowned land surface beneath the sea in front of it.

The purpose of these great stone avenues is completely unknown. There are many burial mounds associated with them, as there are around Stonehenge; but that does not say that the rows had anything to do with burial. If there was any religious purpose in their construction, surely it implies a population much more of the order of that today than one of scattered and primitive farmers? One would have thought that the whole population of Brittany in those days would not have provided a fitting congregation.

We will leave Carnac for the moment and return to Britain. I have already mentioned the stone rows on Dartmoor. Of course these are in no way comparable to the massed avenues at Carnac, but they are reasonably impressive and there are quite a number of them dotted about the moor. I have taken the approximate bearings of eight of them and projected these lines to see what happens. It was obvious at once that the one at Black Tor when projected cuts another row at Warren House, in an area seamed and scarred with very ancient tin workings. It may be a coincidence, but these two lines could have given you a cross-bearing on rich deposits of tin, long before maps are supposed to have existed. In any case how did anybody know that there was tin in Britain without long and elaborate prospecting? I have never liked theories based on ideas of projected lines, but it is curious nevertheless. If there is anything at all in the beacon idea, this gives it some confirmation.

The two rows mentioned are not the only suggestive ones. That at Sharp Tor when produced runs very close to Avebury itself. Those at Fernworthy, Chagford and Higher White Tor hit the great monolith on the summit of Exmoor near The Chains. None of this is quite exact according to modern measurements, but if you were making observations in an unknown and unmapped land, they would be remarkably good. It may all be nonsense, or it may not. But if it is nonsense something will turn up to show that it is.

It has been hinted that Carnac might be the most important place in the whole system. If so, and if there is anything in the idea at all, one at least of the stone rows on Dartmoor should give an approximate bearing on Carnac. Actually three do, the double row on Headland Warren and the single ones at Dartmeet and Butterdon.

I do not even suggest that this idea of bio-electronic beacons is the right answer. All I am trying to demonstrate is that there is something here which could possibly fit into a picture of ancient exploration which we know nothing about. If there is anything in this clue, it is not related to ordinary exploration by sea and land, but concerns something carried out by air transport. This would have seemed utter rubbish a generation ago, but is it quite so absurd today?

The problem of the stone circles and alignments is really one proper to the old world although others are known, particularly in Peru. The new world has others of its own. For instance, what are we to make of the remarkable animal mounds found in considerable numbers to the south and west of the Great Lakes? The Indians have no idea who made them and there seems to be little archaeological evidence for their date. The largest of these appears to be the great Serpent Mound of Adams Country, Ohio. The mound is five feet high on a thirty foot base and if straightened out would be more than a thousand feet, say three hundred metres, long. The work necessary to produce a mound of this size is great and what possible purpose was it intended to serve? Seen from the ground it is nothing but a bank. Only from above is its serpentine form obvious. It is the same with the tortoise, alligator, eagle, lizard, elk, bear, otter, wolf and frog mounds, while some apparently represent human beings.

When once the possibility of the stone circles and alignments of the old world having been used as beacons for aerial navigation has entered one's mind, the same possibility can be appreciated with regard to the animal mounds of the United States. However, in their case the beacons would only be visual ones, unless there was some method of charging them with bio-electronic force. This is not so impossible as most people would think today.

Three

In some of my earlier books I have often remarked that all over the world there seem to be traces of customs and beliefs which appear to indicate that mankind as a whole once knew many things which he has forgotten now. The studies of anthropology and folk-lore are full of such scraps of evidence and more is to be found in comparative religion.

Some of these bits of information have been collected in very unexpected places. Quite recently a French expedition spent a considerable time on Easter Island in the Pacific. The wife of the leader, Francis Mazière, was a Polynesian herself and spoke the language of the native population. Few anthropologists have had this advantage. They may have learnt to speak a native language fluently, but still remained foreigners. Mrs Mazière, though coming from a different island, Tahiti, was able to discuss and record ancient beliefs of the Easter Islanders as one of themselves. Some of these beliefs were very odd indeed. I have taken the following list directly from Mazière's book, *Mysteries of Easter Island*:

(a) The inhabitants of Jupiter have settled the concordance of the planets.
(b) The first planet that man will come to know is Venus.
(c) Our bodies cannot stand more than two months on the planets.
(d) All the planets worship the Sun.
(e) Not many stars are inhabited.
(f) Among us are a people whom we cannot see.

(g) The current and the light of Venus are produced by the air.

(h) Two planets, Jupiter and Mars, have no electricity; they are like the earth. There are no winds.

(i) Only our earth has men of different colours.

(j) There are people living on the Moon.

(k) There is one planet which has no vegetation and no earth; it is made up of water and rocks alone. The sort of human beings who live there are different and they are born in the water. On that planet there are mines of metals unlike our own, especially one unique metal, finer than gold, whose colour is green-black-blue-yellow-red. The planet consists of a ball of rock and iron. The iron crust has to be pierced with a fire of stones to get at the metal. The fire of stones and water brings the metal out very thin. It can be used as cloth.

What is one to make of this astonishing rigmarole? It clearly bothered Mazière himself and he did not like to publish what he thought about it. It is hard to see how it could be a completely blundered interpretation of information about astronomy learnt from a resident priest, although this may be the answer.

There are other strange legends. The Easter Islanders claimed two separate colonizations of the island, the second and more recent having come from the Marquessa group of Hiva two thousand miles north-westward. An earlier one, however, was thought to have come round Cape Horn and to have seen Antarctica far less covered with ice than it is today. A sailing mark was apparently a conspicuous red mountain.

Now to me it seems quite obvious that the famous stone carvings of Easter Island which run into very large numbers and huge weight, are copies in stone of originals cut out of wood. The whole way they are carved points to the manner in which one cuts wood, and not very different wooden figures found in Hiva are still preserved. If you are not very expert in carving figures out of wood, this is how you make them. I used to produce figures like that on a small scale with my first knife as a small boy. Such mystery as there is about the Easter Island carvings is not, I feel, in their appearance, but in the islanders' statements that they were transported and set up by the 'mana',

Figure 7 Reconstruction of an Easter Island statue on its platform and with its hat (based on many photographs and La Pérouse's drawing). Height of the order of 16 feet. Note carving as if in wood.

that is the extra-sensory power, of the king, who was specially trained to develop it. This takes us at once to the world wide belief that such power was available and could be used. If such power can be utilized, surely that is how Stonehenge and other monuments must have been moved and erected? Merlin is said to have done it by marvellous power. Is this very different, except in degree, to the also almost universal stone-throwing trick of the poltergeist, which is frequently reported from all over the old world and the new? A poltergeist is apparently the involuntary mental movement of solid objects by what is now known as telekinesis. If the mind of a somewhat mentally retarded girl can somehow produce numerous wet pebbles from the bed of a stream and throw them about in a house, what could have been done by a mind specially trained to utilize this power?

We don't know the answer to this and many people are either

so incurious, unobservant or deliberately evasive that little is being done to find out. Yet peoples all over the world used to take it as a matter of course. It has often been suggested that the pyramids, in both the new and old worlds, were constructed by this means, instead of by the enormous waste of time and slave labour which would otherwise have been necessary.

What is known about telekinesis, if we must use this depressing technical term? Actually it is probably much more common than most people suppose and frequently passes unnoticed. It may even take place at times in every family and simply be unrecognized as such, for the bulk of modern town dwelling humanity is deplorably unobservant. It was not so in earlier times. Everything out of the ordinary was carefully noticed.

The most obvious demonstration of this power is given in poltergeist cases and here may take the form of objects, often pebbles from a distance, being thrown about, things being set on fire, or bells being rung inexplicably. As an example, a man was once working for me, who some years earlier had been doing a job in my uncle's house of Glenforsa on the Sound of Mull. He was all alone there as an apprentice carpenter. There was nobody else in the house or even nearby. Suddenly all the bells began to ring. He ran to the doors and saw nobody. It went on for a long time and he became quite panic stricken. Now these bells were the old wire kind fastened to cranks. There was no possibility of a short circuit as there is with modern bells. There was nobody ringing them and yet they rang. There are many cases of similar bell ringing recorded. This is an obvious case, but there are much more frequent examples, when something in the house is inexplicably removed or some unexpected object appears where no ordinary circumstance could account for its arrival. We have noticed things of this kind here on many occasions and they can be quite annoying. A library book, for instance, once completely vanished. It was known where it had been put down one day. It could not be found. We had to pay compensation to the library. Weeks later it was noticed on a shelf in a part of the house which was at that time occupied by another family. There was no possible explanation in three-dimensional terms of how it could have got there.

How many people too have not had the experience of a letter vanishing completely? Of course they usually put this down to carelessness on somebody's part, or forgetfulness, or something of that kind. But very often there is no reason to suppose that this is the right answer. Yet it is usually so small a matter that it is passed over as an accident. It is only when poltergeist activity becomes really violent that anybody takes any notice of it and even then they often try to explain it by trickery.

Study of the facts of numerous reported cases of violent polter-

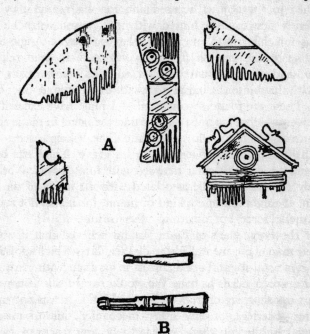

Figure 8 Pagan Anglo-Saxons rid themselves of the 'mana' of the dead. A. Deliberately broken hair-combs. B. Hair tweezers. From many examples found in cremation urns in a cemetery which I excavated at Lackford in Suffolk.

geist activity has led to the conclusion among those who believe in such things that the most frequent origin of the activity is in the mind of some young person, usually female, at the onset of puberty. It is apparently completely involuntary and is thought to be the result of mental strain on the arrival of the sex urge. Whatever the cause, however, you are left with a seemingly impossible problem. How does the mind move these objects about, or set things on fire? This must imply the existence of a force which has not as yet been studied.

Now the existence, or the belief in the possible existence of this force, is well known to the many anthropologists who have spent their working lives studying supposedly backward peoples in out of the way parts of the world and it is spoken of as 'mana'. The people whom they studied knew that a person's mana became attached to the objects he used and for this reason they were frequently destroyed or buried with that person when he died. It was for this reason, no doubt, that the pagan Anglo-Saxon ancestors of the English frequently broke their dead relatives' combs, and other intimate articles, such as hair-tweezers, were put with them into the burial urns with the cremated ashes of the dead. These are found so commonly—I must have excavated at least twenty—that we must assume that the belief in mana spread right across the old world to England. The Vikings used to 'kill' a man's weapons and put them in his grave. The Celts buried his weapons and particular treasures with him. It was all because nobody else wished to be associated with the mana of the dead person. It might become a kind of haunt, for it was not a three-dimensional force, but something otherworldly.

But the Polynesians of Easter Island believed that it was the trained mana, the mental force, of their king which moved the huge stone statues and set them up in position with great stone drums on their heads as hats. We would regard this as nonsense, but for the shortage of trees on Easter Island. It was not easy to produce sheerlegs, or any other mechanical aid to raise the carvings. Neither do there appear to be any traces of earthen ramps, which could have served the same purpose. For that matter there are none at Stonehenge, nor any other megalithic monument that I have seen, although there we have already suggested that the great arches at Stonehenge were raised in the snow. But are we talking nonsense? Is there any such thing as mana? I must say that I existed for quite a long time with a complete disbelief in such a force; now I am not so sure. I rather wonder whether civilized man has not just forgotten how to use it through being so pleased with his other attainments. Even today people still say 'thought is power', although I doubt if many of them know what they mean by this remark.

Now it is possible to demonstrate that there is something in this theory of mana. We have done repeatable experiments with pebbles picked off the beach at Seaton and tested them with a pendulum. A length, the rate, of 24 inches of the cord will react to the handling of a pebble by a male. A rate of 29 inches shows that a female has used it and so on. If the pebbles are picked up with a pair of tongs and then tested one by one, they only react to their chemical composition. But if I take one out and throw it against a wall, it will then respond to the 24 inch male rate. If my wife does the same, the answer is 29 inches for female. This can be repeated as long as you can be bothered to do it. It is a scientific test, in that it is repeatable, and it shows that some unknown property of the man or woman passes from him or her to the stone. This makes the idea of the existence of mana a little less absurd.

But we can take the subject further than this. Round about us here are a number of Iron Age forts on the hill tops. At three of these I have picked up sea rounded flint pebbles precisely similar to those on the local beaches today. But wind and weather do not transport such pebbles up five hundred feet to the top of Sidbury Castle two and a half miles inland, or nine hundred feet up to the fort on Pilsdon Pen five and a half miles from the sea. Man collected these stones, took them up and used them in his slings. All this happened before the birth of Christ, so long ago that it means little to us today.

One would have thought that the temporary impression of mana, or whatever you like to call it, would have washed off the pebbles long, long ago. But this is not the case. All the pebbles I tested with the pendulum reacted to the male rate of 24 inches. But there are other rates as well. There is the rate for age of 30 inches. All these sling-stones from all three camps recorded approximately the same date: 320 B.C. There is also a rate for war. They reacted to that and also to thought.

As it happens I have another collection of sling-stones from Wandlebury Camp, about three miles to the south of Cambridge. Very few of these gave a rate for war and most were presumably used in practice, and all gave the rate for male, except one or two of the less regular examples. The date also was a hundred years later.

This was one of the strangest things I had come across. Mana apparently was extremely long lasting. Was it then mana which gave the effect of an electric shock when we were testing the stones of the Merry Maidens in Cornwall? It seems that it must have been. If so mana is apparently a bio-electronic force and it should be possible to learn a lot about it.

These experiments with pebbles differ from poltergeist phenomena in one important matter. The poltergeist operator does it involuntarily and probably has no idea that he or she is doing it. Our experiments were deliberate. We were trying to see whether we could put anything into the electro-magnetic fields of the stones which could be detected. Call the anything mana if you like; whatever name is given to it, it appears to exist. According to science, the first commandment with promise turns on the question of repeatability. Most so-called psychic, which really means mental, phenomena have been turned down by scientists on this ground. As a matter of interest, very many of the experiments conducted with the pendulum are repeatable and so are those with a divining rod. Therefore, the scientist who continues to deny that anything can be repeated in this branch of study, is simply proving that he is not a scientist but a dogmatist.

Now, if by using such trivial objects as pebbles off the beach you can show that it is possible to alter their electro-magnetic fields by making use of them, what could be learnt if you really got down to years of study of the why and wherefore of it all? Suppose many men through long periods studied it as closely as modern physics has been studied, might not the results be quite astonishing? It seems to me that scraps of evidence all over the world appear to indicate that this has once been done. But was it ever done here? Is it not possible that what now survives is but a fragment of all that could be remembered of what was taught to the local people by our hypothetical explorers, mentioned to some extent already? Were the local people not encouraged to build up the power of the stone circles and other beacon marks by dancing, and had not some explanation been given to them of why it was necessary to do so? Of course this is just a guess, but where did the Kahunas of the Pacific get their learning? There is no anthropological suggestion that Pacific Islanders ever sat down to think out metaphysical ideas for themselves. The teachings of the Kahunas seem to have been derived from a far higher level of civilization than anything ever observed by Europeans when they first made their way into the Pacific. Their control of fire, the forces of nature, of disease and so on and their beliefs in the different levels of man's existence seem to argue a long period of deep reflection and study behind them. The higher self, for instance, is surely something which is only beginning to be glimpsed today by people working on extra-sensory perception; while the lower self seems to have been just touched on by modern students of the subconscious. Yet you get variants of this in many of the older religions, in Buddhism, Brahminism and even Judaism, while the witches of western Europe were said to be able, at one time at any rate, to handle the massed power of thought. Schools appear to have survived for long ages here and there, particularly in the old world, where fragments of a much larger lost lore were still taught. Everywhere we surely see that much more was known once than has persisted till today.

Your higher self, said the Kahunas, if you could get in touch with it, could do anything for you; but you had to be able to contact it. It was not God and you were part of it. In fact it was very like the group soul, whose existence was apparently reported by Myers and others, after their deaths, to the research workers of a generation ago and to the spiritualists of today. It is remarkable that something of the kind can be deduced from a study of the pendulum.

The people who go on explorations are not those who sit down to give themselves over to metaphysical thinking. They may be hardy, competent field workers, observers and mechanics, but may have not yet reached an age at which they are likely to bother much about the whys and wherefores of the universe. Therefore it would be improbable that they would know much more about the bio-electronic force than was necessary for its practical application. Supposing such people had arrived on earth in several expeditions to different areas, what they could pass on to the local inhabitants would be strictly limited and its practical application would probably develop before long into a varied collection of quasi-religious and finally completely religious practices. The natives who learnt most about it would develop into a priesthood, secretly handing on the elements of their knowledge of the use of hidden power. One cannot help thinking that this looks very much like what we actually find. Of course this is still guessing. I am no believer that it happened, yet I do see the possibilities and feel that it is worth more consideration.

This would perhaps be a good point to summarize what we appear to have learnt so far in this book.

We began with a legendary puzzle from the Old Testament: who were the sons of God? It did not seem probable that they were any known people of antiquity. The story of sons or companions of God is, as it happens, not only found in the old world, but is of great age in the new world also. We noticed a possible similarity between these Biblical sons of God and the gods of ancient Greece.

The gods of ancient Greece were remarkable in various ways. There was nothing particularly godlike or respectable about them. They behaved like ordinary men and women on a rather grander scale. There was one great difference, however. These gods flew and they often did so in mechanical contraptions, which the Greeks called chariots. The chief of the gods could also throw thunderbolts to destroy people who annoyed him. The gods could mate and produce fertile children on earthly women. This was also a characteristic of the Biblical sons of God. Of the Greek gods one might fairly say that the descriptions of them are what one would expect to find, had a small modern expedition of both sexes arrived by helicopter among some isolated and backward tribe, who had never heard of flying-machines or hand grenades.

The cross-bred descendants of gods and women, both in the Bible and in Greek mythology, became heroes and giants. The same thing is evident in the later myths and legends of the Germanic peoples of north-west Europe. These are probably not derived from Greek legend but had an independent source.

There is another point to remember: the word for a god in classical times did not necessarily refer to a greatly superhuman being. It was a title which was given on many occasions to living men and became an ordinary designation of the Roman emperors.

To see if it helped in any way with an explanation of the problem, we spent a little time on the controversy over diffusion and independent invention and from this came to Geoffrey of Monmouth's legendary story of the erection of Stonehenge. This is clearly an Irish legend somehow brought over with its Erse names and written into a somewhat fabulous account of the history of the sister island, Britain. It is so interesting that I made an attempt to see whether there could have been any foundation for it and found that it was possible. However, here we came upon a new problem. What was the original purpose in setting up great rings and avenues of stones?

At this point I introduced a study of which many modern scientists do not approve, that of extra-sensory perception. I described how one Cornish stone circle, the Merry Maidens, was still apparently highly charged with what we must assume to be bio-electricity, living electricity. It was suggested that this had probably been done by means of ring dances inside the circle and attention was drawn to ritual ring dances still being performed all over the world. It is known from experiment that such charges as that found in the stones can be detected at very great distances and heights by dowsers using pendulums and other aids.

Here I made a very long and possibly impossible shot. I suggested that these stones had perhaps been deliberately charged, not for any religious purpose which seemed to make no sense, but to serve as navigational beacons from the air. This suggestion is probably quite enough to classify me as a 'nut-case' to many readers. But perhaps they are forgetting the traditional aerial navigation of the Greek and other gods. In fact there is plenty of it recorded in the Bible. It is only in the last few decades that anyone in their senses could have considered the possibility at all; but now, granted the possibility that peoples other than those on Earth might have discovered space travel long before us and been much further advanced in the study of bio-electronics, would not the equivalent of bio-electronic 'radar' beams have been a great help in finding their way about unexplored and densely forested countries?

Leaving the old world, we then spent a little time in the discussion of the enigmatic stone statues on Easter Island in the Pacific. Here it is understood that the islanders believe them to have been transported and set up by what many people today call the 'supernatural' power of the island king. This power is known over much of the far east as mana.

Supernatural is of course a misnomer. Nothing is supernatural except the creator of the universes and I say universes because in the singular the term is often restricted to the single galaxy in which our solar system is located. Mana, whatever it is, must be a natural power, just as ghosts and poltergeists must be natural phenomena. To be supernatural you have to be almighty.

We then glanced briefly at the meaning of mana. This is not

only a power which is believed to be able to move huge weights and set them in upright positions without gear or tackle. It is also some detached portion of a living personality, which can become attached to an inanimate object and survive in that object the death of its owner. We saw that in earlier times the belief in mana extended all over Europe as far as the British Isles.

Next I described experiments with stones from the beach and showed to my own satisfaction that it could be demonstrated in a scientific manner that some portion of a personality could indeed be detached and permanently fixed in the field of such an inanimate object as a beach pebble. The experiments were repeated at least a hundred times and could be done so indefinitely. So we then saw that there was nothing absurd in the mana of numbers of people excited by vigorous dancing becoming fixed in the stones of the Merry Maidens, where it was detected very much later by the use of a pendulum.

We end this chapter then with some conviction that there is indeed a bio-electronic force, which for want of a better term we will call mana, and this can be used, as it were, to electrify stone monuments in a manner in which their position can be detected high in the skies above. The point, however, now becomes more important. Could there have been anyone flying in these skies, who could detect these supposed beacons?

Four

For most of my life the answer to the question at the end of the last chapter would have been : 'Of course not.' Still, during this time the first man has flown across the channel; the first men have flown across the Atlantic and the first men have landed on the moon. The moon and Mars have been shown to be different from what all the expert astronomers expected and nobody knows what may be found on other planets of the solar system, itself only a minute dot in the whole galaxy in which it is situated. It would be a very pig-headed man today who could say that humanity on Earth is the highest intelligence anywhere in the galaxy, and who could contend that it is impossible for more advanced races to exist somewhere in it. If there should happen to be more advanced civilizations somewhere, why should they not have produced machines to eliminate space. Every year Earth machines travel faster and there is no reason to suppose that the limit of speed has been nearly attained. I can remember when it was authoritatively claimed that it was impossible to exceed the speed of sound without a machine flying to pieces. In fact, in spite of all the bluster and back slapping, very little is really known. Our wonders of applied science are just scratchings at the surface of things.

Let us go back for a moment to the extraordinary list of legendary information collected by Mrs Mazière on Easter Island. Could these be simply products of the islanders' imagination? If not, then where on earth did they come from? The Sixth statement, 'Among us are a people whom we cannot see' can be ignored for the moment, as probably referring to ghosts, which play a greater part in the lives of isolated peoples than they do in urban civilizations. There are such things as ghosts, and we have seen examples, but they appear in most cases to be no more than a natural equivalent of television, sound and vision. However, the rest of the list refers to other planets in such a way that it seems most difficult to see how it could be simple supposition. Neither does it appear easy to see how it could be a misunderstanding of recent teachings about astronomy.

There are then at least two very strange things about Easter Island. The first, and most obvious, is the mass of great stone statues, weighing up to as much as fifty tons, set up, we are told, by mana and thus presumably suitable as a direction beacon, if such things existed. The second is an extraordinary list of scraps of information about the planets, which could have been derived from people who really did know something about them. The information may be entirely incorrect, but nobody here today is in a position to know.

However, Easter Island has also a creation myth, which is worth considering. (The great god of the universe is known as Make-Make.) Mazière records this myth as follows:

Make-Make rolled earth into a ball, thrust his hand into the middle of it to make a hole, then breathed into the hole. A young man, He Repa, came out of it. Make-Make said, 'This is not right!' He made He Repa sleep. Make-Make took a banana shoot. He opened He Repa's chest on the left-hand side. The blood flowed on to the banana shoot. Make-Make breathed into the shoot running with blood. Uka, the young woman, was born.

Well, we were brought up on a story like this (Genesis 2, verse 7, etc.)

And the Lord God formed man of the dust of the ground, and breathed into his nostrils the breath of life; and man became a living soul. (v. 7)

And Adam gave names to all cattle, and to the fowl of the air, and to every beast of the field; but for Adam there was not found an help meet for him. (v. 20)

And the Lord caused a deep sleep to fall on Adam, and he

slept : And he took one of his ribs, and closed up the flesh
instead thereof; and the rib which the Lord God had taken
from man, made he a woman, and brought her unto the
man. (v. 21–2)

Now these two stories, the Easter Island myth and the Biblical
one, are clearly the same. But where did the Easter Islanders get
their version? The obvious answer is that the supposedly Polynesian creation myth is later than contact with Europeans. A
Dutchman, Roggeveen, named the island in 1722. There has been
contact ever since and the natives, who had suffered many
massacres, transportations and other afflictions, were converted to
Christianity by a resident priest, Eugene Eyraud, who arrived
there in 1863. This gives at least a hundred years for Adam and
Eve to become He Repa and Uka. It all looks quite simple. One
has known that even in respectable Huntingdonshire the name
Flagholms became the Lagoons in a similar passage of years.

If this is the right explanation, then the story of the early
migration round the south of Patagonia may be a reflection also
of the first European voyages and the conspicuous red hill be the
well-known Cape Horn, the Cape Stiff of sailors, and not on
Antarctica at all. But there is a difficulty in the way of accepting
this reasonable explanation. In pre-Spanish-American writings
there is a similar story of humanity being created out of mud, by
entities who resemble rather closely the Biblical sons of God.
There is the same general picture, too, of the earlier experiments
being a failure and the destruction of these earlier men by their
creators. Neither in the Biblical version nor in the American one
is God depicted as being alone in His creative work; for in the
Bible He is said to have remarked: 'Let *us* make man in *our*
image.'

Of course when men move about the world on the oceans many
things move with them in a seemingly inexplicable way. The boat
balers of Polynesia in the Pacific are exactly like those used by the
old Viking boatmen in western Europe and the anchors found
with Caligula's house-boats in Lake Nemi in Italy like those still
used by Chinese junks and nowhere else. It is just possible that
these creation stories reached America by early Irish monastic
voyages or, as some think, by actual Christian missionaries. But
it is hardly probable that this is the correct explanation.

I have for years been interested in early crossings of the Atlantic and for a long time have thought that Irish monks, as typified in the stories of St Brendan, had probably reached America long before the Vikings went there. However I do not set much store by the Quetzalcoatl legends as some people interpret them today. Whatever their interpretation may be, I doubt that Quetzalcoatl was an Irish monk and certainly not a Norse explorer.

It is interesting to examine this question of early voyages to America in some detail, for much has been written about them and very little is really known. If, for instance, it could be shown that a medieval Welsh prince, Madoc, had really taken a large expedition over to America about A.D. 1170, it could explain how creation myths might filter into many areas before the Spaniards came. If, too, Brendan made the voyages ascribed to him and found Celtic Christian monks already settled there, it could perhaps explain the Quetzalcoatl legends.

In 1961 C. M. Boland published in America a book entitled *They All Discovered America* which dealt with many of these supposed adventures in a popular form and is useful to the general reader. However there is a gap in knowledge between the archaeologists of Europe and those in America. Few of us know American archaeology at all well and still less is known of our material on the other side of the Atlantic. For this reason a number of things quoted by Boland as concrete evidence of settlers from Europe in the other continent will not pass in our eyes. But this is not the case in Boland's supposed traces of Madoc's Welshmen.

There has been doubt as to whether the original story was not a deliberate fake instigated by Henry VII, when he was employing men to research into his pedigree to justify his claim to the English crown after the defeat and death of Richard III at Bosworth Field. Though this seems an improbable explanation. A Welsh bard named Gutton Owen is said to have found the story in the archives of Conway Abbey and told it to Hakluyt who included it in his *Voyages* in the reign of Elizabeth I. The idea that it was a fake is based on the theory that Elizabeth could use Madoc's supposed settlement to claim her right to the sovereignty as it preceded that of the Spaniards by several hundred years. Hakluyt actually says this himself, but it is most unlikely that the story had no foundation in fact. Madoc's ancestry is known and it seems evident that he did make a voyage of exploration to the west. According to Hakluyt, writing in about 1580, Madoc left most of his people in America in A.D. 1170 and returned to Wales for more colonists. All this can be read in Hakluyt's *Voyages*, which have been published frequently since Elizabeth's day. Whether Madoc really returned with ten shiploads of followers, nobody really knows.

There is nothing improbable about Madoc's voyage of discovery. Wales has always produced adventurous seamen and it is only just across the Irish Sea from the Pale of Dublin, where many tales no doubt circulated about strange countries overseas. Dublin, when the Vikings ruled it, received an embassy from Spain. Norsemen from Iceland and probably from Greenland fought at Clontarf outside its walls, against the native Irish. It is more than probable that by Madoc's day the voyages to America of Leif Ericsson, Thorfinn Karlsefni and the rest were commonplace wharfside talk in Dublin. In monastic circles the expeditions attributed to St Brendan, supposedly sailing from Ireland itself, must have been well known. To say that Madoc could not have known of the existence of America is manifestly wrong. People who think that obviously have no idea how fond sailors are of a yarn. I think it is only just to include Madoc on the list of early voyagers across the North Atlantic. But when we come to the rest of the tale, it is a different story. Boland, and I seem to recall others before him who had the same idea, thinks that Madoc's colonists became the ancestors of the now extinct Mandan Indians. The Indians died out from imported European diseases, but before they did so there were people who knew them who claimed that Welsh speakers could appreciate many Welsh words in their language. There may be some truth in this, although other authorities have suggested that the Mandans were survivors of the Greenland Norse colonists who had migrated to America when the climate deteriorated in their first settlements. However the Mandans were located in an unexpected area for the second idea to be probable. They lived far up the Missouri above St Louis. Boland suggests that the colonists first arrived in the Gulf of Mexico, sailed up the Mississippi to its junction with the Ohio and up that again to Louisville where he locates their permanent settlement on Sand Island. Here they apparently went native and became white Indians. They were driven out of this area and migrated once more down the Ohio and up the Missouri. It is said that skeletons and armour of the white Indians are to be found on Sand Island but nobody can be bothered to test the supposition.

The evidence in favour of Welsh having been spoken by the Mandans is considerable and contemporary with the Indian troubles of the European settlers before the War of Independence down to the extinction of the tribe by disease. They were supposed to have had a Welsh copy of the Bible carefully preserved. One point has not, as far as I have seen, been mentioned anywhere. Welshmen would have had a far greater chance than Norsemen of establishing themselves among the Indians of America, for they were the inventors of the longbow and could outshoot the Indian bow.

It is a strange story, almost too remarkable to be the result of indiscriminate chatter. Too many Welsh-speaking settlers remarked on the Welsh language of the Mandans. Why should they have imagined it? But if Boland's interpretation of the evidence is correct, and I feel it might well be so, then there could have been Christians in some numbers not so very far distant by, say, the Red river from the Inca lands in Mexico. There could have been Welsh missionaries, and the Welsh are rather prone to this kind of thing, drifting over to the west and teaching versions of Bible tales wherever they went, hundreds of years before the Spanish invasion and conquest. To know how large this possibility is, someone surely ought to find out what kind of people were buried on Sand Island. What better time than now, when we have a Welsh-speaking achaeologist as Prince of Wales?

Boland was not so happy with some of his other suppositions. He suggested the former existence of settlers from the Roman world, Christians flying from persecution, who settled in Virginia. In support of this he gave as evidence a large collection of iron and other objects found at a place called Jeffress high up the Roanoke river.

There are iron nails, wedges and roves for rivets, blacksmith wrought material of any date from the birth of Christ to A.D. 1850 or later. But the king pin of this collection was a bronze cup with a foot like a candlestick, which he claimed was similar to six found in the ash filled ruins of Pompeii. I was not sure of the date of this cup, but did not think it was Roman, and so tried it on Sir Thomas Kendrick, the former head of the British Museum whose knowledge is much wider than mine. His answer was that it was a post-Reformation chalice. In fact it had belonged to a community of early 16th–17th century settlers. I was not surprised. The heads of the iron nails were smaller than most Roman ones I had found. But here you see the archaeological difficulty. There are not many people in England who have even seen a bronze chalice of this period. There are few, if any, in America, and as the study of archaeology becomes more and more specialized, it becomes far harder to find people with general knowledge and wide learning. Even before I left Cambridge, more than a dozen years ago, people were coming to me for this kind of information and mine is very limited compared with that of the older race of archaeologists. In fact the more specialized archaeology becomes, the less it appears to be able to find out. If you cannot tell the rusted lever of a Mill's grenade from a Roman barrel-lock key, or a gouge from a shoehorn, how can you expect to deal with the trivial objects a dig usually produces? No one is fit for a specialized degree in archaeology until he has spent at least a year just handling and observing things of all periods in a big museum. Many of the degrees given today are often not worth the paper they are written on; for the lecturers themselves do not know enough, and much of what they teach could easily be mugged up from publications by the students themselves without going near a lecture room. I suspect that this is true of many other subjects also and this cry for higher pay for teachers comes from parrots not getting as many sunflower seeds as they would like. The question really is : 'Are so many parrots needed?' For what is really necessary is to excite young people to think and work out problems for themselves and not to just cram them with undigested facts for an examination.

My object in writing books is just this, to stimulate people to think, observe and experiment for themselves and not to just swallow the sayings of authorities of the time as if these were the Word of God. Nobody knows very much and there is not a person living today who is in a position to refute the extraordinary statements about the planets recovered from the legends of Easter Island. It does not seem probable that there are people living on the moon as the Easter Islanders believe; but there may be ghosts of those who once lived there, or some people on another level of vibration.

If one does much research work on ESP (the commonly used contraction for extra-sensory perception), it becomes increasingly obvious, much as one may doubt it at the start, that there are other levels of existence beyond the one with which we are familiar and that people live on these levels. In other books I have reported how our knowledge about such matters has been to some extent enlarged, and I will not recapitulate it now, though I will say once again that it is possible for most people to learn about it for themselves. Not everyone can do so, for there are a few whose bio-electronic voltage is not high enough. Many there are, however, who are too bigoted, lazy or unscientific to make the attempt.

It is this question of people living on different levels of vibration which can put another interpretation on the Easter Islanders' statement that there are people living among us whom we cannot see. These may not just be ghosts but living entities whose vibrations are so fast that they are beyond our light spectrum scale, in which case the islanders knew more about it than the bulk of civilized mankind. Their belief would then not be absurd at all, but a reasonable piece of information.

Quetzalcoatl was, or as there were several, the Quetzalcoatls were like the typical early gods elsewhere who introduced metal working, agriculture and suchlike useful crafts. They were revered apparently by Toltecs, Mayas and Incas. The interesting thing about the legends is that one Quetzalcoatl introduced people from abroad who could not speak the native languages and he also introduced the worship of a single great god. He departed eastward over the sea after promising that he would return again. It was Montezuma the Inca king's hesitation and doubt over whether the Spaniards were arriving with Quetzalcoatl or not which led to the conquest of Mexico. The whole series of legends is very confused and it is doubtful whether anything can be made of the often supposed European ancestry and possibly Christian teaching of this man or men. The date is believed to be somewhere in the early eleventh century.

Sometimes it is pointed out that there are Inca carvings of men showing European features and I have indeed seen one, which would have passed for a Hellenistic statuette from northern

India, were it not for the fact that the eyes are not shown and are only represented by pits. I do not really believe that much certainty can be based on the Quetzalcoatl legends, except that here, as in the Bible and elsewhere, you find a story of a superhuman teacher often of rather different physical characteristics to those of the people among whom he appeared.

Much has been talked in recent years about a puzzling archaeological site at North Salem in New England. Some would see this as a former settlement of Irish monks and even earlier visitors. It is in the role of a later generation Irish settler that Boland imagines the missionary Quetzalcoatl. I am afraid I cannot see much resemblance to anything of Celtic type at North Salem. There is one conspicuous object which is often published as an altar stone. To me this large stone resembles something well known in the English West Country. It looks like the floor stone, or bed, of a cider press; with grooves round the edges to catch the juice running out of the apples as they are crushed. But I may be quite wrong. Perhaps I do know the European side of Celtic Christian archaeology as well as most authorities, but I know very little about any American archaeology except that of the Eskimo. I do not know enough to guess at the possible origin of the Quetzalcoatl legends, but do doubt very much that there was anything Christian about it all. It seems possible that the whole affair was very much older and that Quetzalcoatl was some genuine high god of a much earlier age.

Five

No one can accuse me of being unduly sceptical about the possibilities of early crossings of the North Atlantic. I have written quite a lot about them and was indeed the instigator of Frank Glynn's search for the Westford knight. I do not believe necessarily that it was one of Sinclair's followers whose effigy was pecked out, probably by the expedition's armourer, on that New England rock slab. In fact I have a fancy that the effigy represents a somewhat earlier Scotsman who possibly bears MacDonald arms on his shield. But I do believe that expeditions to North America were quite frequent once land to the west had been firmly fixed in the minds of northern Europeans. It would be strange if this were not so. The settlers in Greenland had no timber and it was to be had for the cutting and transport only a relatively short sea passage away. It was much less risk and trouble than fetching it from Europe, as is done today. Of course they went and it is very strange to me that Americans as a whole take so little interest in it.

I think too that there is a lot of tradition at the back of the St Brendan stories and even perhaps in the earlier pagan beliefs in a happy land, Tir nan Og, far to the west. Someone must have seen the fogs and the fish on the Grand Banks of Newfoundland as reported in St Brendan's story. These banks were known to the Basque fishermen long before the days of Columbus. The volcanoes of Iceland also figure in it. But surely this is really a collection of travellers' tales and not a report of two voyages of one saint. It is much like the way scraps of truth got into the mythical history of Geoffrey of Monmouth which we have already met.

However, if you are writing a series of sailors' yarns up into a life of a saint who perhaps had made some lengthy voyage of discovery, you have to build it into some kind of consecutive account and cook your sailing directions to fit it. The warm and fertile islands which Brendan was supposed to have visited could well be from the story of some other navigator's voyage to the Azores and not to America at all.

What we can really say is that at the time Brendan's story was written down in the two versions, 'the Life' in the Book of Lismore and 'the Metrical Life', something was known of Iceland, Newfoundland and warmer islands and lands somewhere in the southwest. Brendan's two voyages were supposedly between A.D. 519 and 527. But the earliest surviving account is the *Navigatio Brendani*, written apparently in the eleventh century, when Norsemen had already been in Greenland for a considerable time and had seen the coast of America. The Lives of Brendan cannot really be used as evidence that the Irish were in America before the Norsemen. The name of the first European who is known to have seen the continent is Bjarni Herjulfsson, who on a voyage to Greenland (somewhere about A.D. 990) was blown off his course as far as that. He took so little interest in what he saw that he did not bother to land and was much abused by Eric the Red, who had already colonized Greenland, for this neglect. Eric's son, Leif, about ten years later, did go and spend some months ashore. This is as well known as most early history can be. Yet we find that the majority of Americans today credit Columbus, who never landed on the continent at all and only reached the Caribbean Islands, five hundred years after Bjarni Herjulfsson saw the continent, with having discovered their land! How remarkable this is. In a few hundred years' time who will be given the credit for the first landing on the moon? The Chinese perhaps.

Although what I have just written does make the idea of settlements of Irish monks in New England seem impossible, it by no means denies the possibility of their former existence. The early Celtic monks were continually searching for deserts in which to meditate. It was a widespread fashion of the early Dark Ages and parties went to meditate in the real deserts of Africa also. There is a strong resemblance between the early Christian art of Ethiopia and that of Celtic Britain, which is not generally observed. The first discoverer of Greenland was apparently a

Scottish monk named Cormac, who went there generations before Eric the Red. Others may well have gone further and lived out their lives in Tir nan Og. But if they did, nothing has yet been found to prove it and very little is likely to remain which could do so.

It is not monks who are likely to have left tangible evidence of their arrival and stay, for their lives were dedicated to poverty. The traces to be looked for are those of men living normal lives who used plenty of objects and built houses to make themselves comfortable. There is more chance of finding signs of Madoc's men than of all the monks who may ever have crossed the ocean. If too they brought no women with them, it is easy to see how they could rapidly have become White Indians. By barter or capture, they would have provided themselves with wives and each generation become more Indian than the last. I do not know, but it would be interesting to learn whether the Mandans used iron arrow heads. If they did, while most of the other tribes used stone in early times, then I would strongly suspect that their bowmen had Welsh in their ancestry. The Welsh longbow arrow head was a barbed iron one with a one inch longer socket. I have found a few in Wales of about the time of Madoc, but of course they have mostly rusted away. Of all things that Madoc's settlers' children would be most loath to give up, I fancy that their efficient iron arrow heads would come first. The longbow was Wales' great medieval invention and could drive an arrow, so Giraldus Cambrensis says, four inches through an oak door. He said he had seen their points still sticking through the castle door at Abergavenny six years after the siege.

Yet, as I have said before, it is difficult for Americans to get information such as this. There is, as far as I know, no book readily available on either side of the Atlantic which gives answers of this kind. It is far easier to learn facts about the earlier Stone, Bronze, Iron and Roman times, than to get reasonable information about the medieval. One does not like to comment on the reason for this, but isn't it obvious that, as the study becomes more complicated, fewer people wish to spend the necessary time in working at it? In the archaeology of the Bronze Age, for instance, it is relatively easy for an intelligent person to learn all there is to know about the pots and implements of western Europe. By medieval times it has all become so complicated that few dare to tackle it at all. When I worked at Cambridge at the Anglo-Saxon period, there were at most half a dozen scholars in that field who all knew each other. Scholars of the medieval period in England today may perhaps be as many, but I can only think of four. It is on the publications of these few that what little teaching there is, is based. Anyone who has anything to do with the subject knows how unsatisfactory this is. Television films and such like reconstructions are usually ridiculously inaccurate. The required knowledge simply is not there. Not long ago there was a long and elaborate production of *Hereward the Wake*, which was widely hailed as a marvel. Knowing a little about the period, there was hardly an object portrayed in use which was correct. Even the swords were wrong and these are comparatively well known. If this is so in England, where there is a great mass of medieval material for study, how can the Americans learn anything about it, in a country where none is as yet recognized? It is more difficult for them, than for us to learn the archaeology of Incas, or Toltecs.

However all this talk is only an attempt to see how the Bible story of Adam and Eve could possibly have reached Easter Island before the days of European visits. It has really no connection with the main problems of the book, for there is an immense stretch of time between the eleventh century of our era and the period when the remarks about the sons of God were written into the Bible. The odds against any Bible story having first reached the Incas and then somehow become transported to Easter Island are so great that we can really disregard the possibility.

Yet there does appear to be some artistic link between Easter Island and the American mainland. It seems to be considerably older than the great stone statues. If there was contact at some unknown time, then perhaps the creation story is an American Indian one and not from the Bible at all. Are all these stories in fact much older than they appear to be and could they have been learnt from an entirely different source? What about this story of Atlantis for instance?

Now it is an observable fact that there is much more water in the sea today than there was in classical times. And it is in the classics that the existence and drowning of Atlantis are mentioned. Actually there are many foundered lands around the continents of the world, which could be claimed as the site of Atlantis. Even in our own North Sea, Heligoland has been claimed as a remnant of Atlantis. Or you might choose the sunken ground of Lyonnesse round the Scillies, Vil d'Ys off Brittany and so on. There were wide lands not long ago in geological times where the trawlers work the Dogger Bank, and up in the trawls come the hunting weapons of Mesolithic man, the bones of wild cattle and remains of plants common in England today. Much has been drowned and there is no evidence that the process is finished. Britain goes up and down through the millennia like a see-saw.

But the tradition about Atlantis is that it had a higher civilization than the Europe of its day and there was talk of flying machines and such like advanced mechanical devices. Was there an Atlantis or is it a figment of Greek imagination? One thing is clear. It was outside the Mediterranean, beyond the Pillars of Hercules, the Straits of Gibraltar. It is no use expecting to find it overwhelmed by some volcanic eruption in the Mediterranean itself. Such civilizations there appear to be, but, by definition, they cannot have been Atlantis. However Atlantis may be another name for Tarshish, or Tartessos, which lay between two rivers in southern Spain and was said to have had six thousand years of written history well before the birth of Christ.

The difficulty with all this is one we have met before; the absence of any material relics of such civilizations. There may have been a Silver Man who ruled Tartessos and he may have survived in Celtic mythology as Lugh of the Silver Arm. Tartessos, or Atlantis, may have stood where the shoals lie off Cape Trafalgar today, or they may have been out round the Azores where Carthaginian coins are reported to have been found. We just know nothing about it. But if there were highly advanced Atlantians, or Tartessians, where are their abandoned spanners and bully beef tins? Did they just do everything by mana and need no tools at all? It seems very unlikely. It seems most improbable that no relic of these supposed civilizations would have come into the hands of archaeologists by now and been at once identified as something belonging to an entirely unknown culture. Archaeologists all over the world exchange information. Someone by now would have said: 'We have a very odd object in the museum. It's quite unlike anything we have ever seen. Do you know what it is?' This is often happening and usually somebody knows the answer, or can get as near as saying: 'Well, it's rather like those things from so and so.' I have had this experience often and the most unlikely people may supply the answer.

I can give an example to explain what I mean. During the 1930s, I had a number of small digs on Late Saxon sites round Cambridge, and we were able to identify the general forms of the pots in use at that period. But every now and then, amid the sherds of unglazed vessels, a scrap would turn up of a fine light yellow glaze which seemed quite foreign to the rest. I assumed that they were imports from some distant land and I was greeted with howls of disbelief when I told people, who thought they knew, that I was finding yellow glazed Late Saxon pottery. Glaze was assumed dogmatically to have not come into use in England till long after the Norman Conquest.

After the Hitler war, we had a visit one day from R. B. K. Stevenson from the Edinburgh museum. After talking to him for a time, I asked him if he was interested in Late Saxon pottery. He was. I showed him ordinary specimens and then one or two of the yellow glaze. He recognized the glaze at once. Some years earlier he had been digging at the royal palace of Byzantium. The glaze was common there and he knew it well. The shapes of the pots were quite different, but the glaze was the same. Someone, probably a high ecclesiastic, had sent to Byzantium for a potter, who knew how to glaze the local pots. It only needed the know-how of a single man. It still took several years before we were believed, but Byzantine glazes on Late Saxon pots are well established now.

This kind of meeting between archaeologists and their mutual exchange of knowledge must inevitably have drawn attention to examples of things of Atlantian manufacture unless they are incredibly rare. Irish gold ornaments have been identified in Palestine; Egyptian beads and Greek ornaments in southern England; ivories from the Middle East in Spain or Irish bronzes from the bottom of Cadiz harbour. Yet, as far as I know, no single enigmatic object which could possibly be thought to have originated in Atlantis has ever turned up.

The legend of Atlantis comes from Plato in the *Timaeus*. He got it from the writings of Solon who was told it by priests in Egypt. Therefore it is third hand at the very best. Briefly the story is this: Atlantis was a large island, bigger than Asia Minor and Libya combined and just outside the Pillars of Hercules. A host of lesser islands lay beyond it. Thus it was well over a thousand miles to the westward of islands now suggested as a possible site for it in the eastern Mediterranean. Atlantis, according to Solon's tale, had been a powerful country nine thousand years before his birth and its armies had overwhelmed all countries around the Mediterranean except Athens. If there were any truth in this, it would mean that there was an extensive and organized civilization off the western end of the Mediterranean at a time when the population of Europe consisted of nothing more than small and scattered hunting and fishing tribes to whom the use of metal was unknown. Plato in his *Critias* described the ideal commonwealth of Atlantis; but nobody has ever been able to decide whether he made all this up himself, or whether some of it came from the Egyptian priests.

Atlantis was ultimately swallowed by the sea and nothing remained in Plato's day save impassable shoals.

Of course this is a most intriguing problem and has occupied the thoughts of many men throughout the ages. Was there any such place at all? The only point in confirmation of the whole story is that there are shoals on both shores, the Spanish and the African coasts, close outside the Straits of Gibraltar. Men now fish for green lobsters on the African shoals, but I have never heard of anyone pulling up an Atlantean goblet in a trawl. Perhaps nobody has enough interest to keep a look out for such a thing.

However it has been frequently noticed that there is a resemblance between the story of Atlantis and other legendary lost lands; such as the Breton land of Ys; the Cornish Lyonnesse; Avalon; Tir nan Og and so on. They may well all refer to one lost land, or each one may be distinct from the others. As we have noticed before, there is much more water in the sea than there was in the Bronze Age. At the back of one's mind too, there is the curious resemblance between the stone axes of the eastern Mediterranean area, the little female figurines, and their counterparts on the Caribbean Islands. The supposed Atlantis would come nearly half way between the two groups, though there may be a great difference in the actual dating of the sets of objects.

Like many legends, there is something true behind this tale, even if we cannot yet see what it is. Presumably the dating of

Atlantis is wrong, the height of its civilization is incorrect and the extent of its conquests greatly exaggerated. Athens had no part in the story. Yet the whole thing may be a garbled memory of the exploits of the Megalithic builders, or even of a people who set them to build. There may have been some important base on low islands outside the Pillars of Hercules.

Six

Now I will bring in a new puzzle, even if I seem to be involving the reader in the imagination of space travel. As before, I do not know the answer, but it is evident to me that an answer could be found and ought to be sought, even if the seeker may be greeted with ridicule by those who have not the imagination to look for it. Of course I refer to the huge and growing mass of statements, often by highly competent eye-witnesses, that strange flying objects are frequently seen in the sky. These are known widely now as UFOs, unidentified flying objects.

I have no personal experience of this kind. Or, to be more accurate, the only experience I have ever had was not of a kind to inspire belief in visitors from another planet or anything of that nature. I had better report it because it is an example of how difficult this kind of observation can be. It was in the summer of 1931 and I had been down to visit my sons at school near Fareham on the Solent. I was driving back, alone in the car, to spend a night or two with my mother at Bracknell before returning to Cambridge. When nearing Alton I ran into a very heavy rainstorm. It was so heavy I turned my lights on and dropped into low gear. I doubt whether the car was moving at ten miles an hour.

On approaching Alton, I rounded a bend and was looking down a lane on my left side. There were bushes and then a wall on its far side. Above the middle of the lane, apparently about twelve feet up, was a great shining disc or globe, which appeared far bigger than the moon as we see it from the earth. Not knowing exactly where the thing was as there was no visible background, I estimated its size as roughly three feet across. It was much the same colour as the moon seen on a clear night and it was slowly descending towards the road. The edges of the object were not distinct, but in any case the rain was too heavy for them to appear so. Of course it did not take me many seconds to pass the end of the lane, but at its apparent rate of descent it might have hit the ground almost directly after I had passed. Of course I ought to have stopped the car, got out and gone to see whether there was any sign of it. There might have been a mark on the road or even a hole in it. But there was no bang. It was very wet and I had no coat handy. I drove thoughtfully on. I did not know what I had seen.

On reaching my mother's house, my story was greeted with obvious disbelief. So was it at Cambridge, except for one person who said it was ball-lightning. So it may have been, but what is that? I do not think this was one of the things called UFOs, or flying saucers, but to this day no one has given me a plausible explanation. My own idea was that it was an incandescent ball of gas. As far as I could judge, its circumference was a perfect circle. It was not a tilted disc or anything of that kind.

That is my sole personal experience of unknown objects in the sky. But I have had some practice which may perhaps help me in considering the reported experiences of other people. In the summer of 1937, I helped physicists studying cosmic rays to let up and plot the course of fairly large balloons on the west coast of Greenland. Thus I have a very good idea of what such things look like at varying heights. For instance I know that once you lose the image of a weather balloon in the field of your theodolite at as low a height as five thousand feet, it is most difficult to pick up the minute dot in the sky again. The objects which people report must be very large indeed.

John Lorne Campbell, who is a well-known scholar and author, is also laird of Canna in the small isles off the west of Scotland. Some years ago he showed me on a projector a colour cinema film of an object, which appeared high in the sky above the opposite isle of Sanday. People had said that this was a weather balloon. The object was clearly at a considerable height as could be judged by the height of the cliffs beneath it. It was a shining disc, but not a perfect circle. Whatever the thing was, I do not think that it can have been smaller than a tennis court and probably much larger. It had remained there almost stationary for a long time.

What, too, was I to think of a visit from a well-known Honiton merchant who came here to tell me that he had watched through a small telescope the evolutions of a number of objects like wheels in the sky? He obviously believed he had seen them and had seen them also changing formation and performing various exercises.

Now people may exaggerate and they may mistake what they think they see. I have seen photographs in the papers, which look as if they had been the shades of Tilley lamps and I have read accounts which were obviously distortions of the real facts. However there is a large residuum, which clearly needs an explanation. People as a whole report truly what they have seen to the best of their ability.

A recent announcement on the BBC news makes it obvious that something needs investigation. As far as I can now remember the radio said that the American Air Force was closing down a department formed to investigate reports on UFOs. They had examined thousands of reports of sightings and there were only about seven hundred which they could not explain. Good heavens, could any official department expect to be able to get away with that? Seven hundred unexplained cases of what might be visitors from another planet, and it was not worth the trouble and expense of trying to find out what they were! Suppose you had many reports that there were thousands of spies in your country and of these only seven hundred could not be shown to be innocent, what would you think of a government which gave up vetting them? If correctly reported, this must surely be one of the most naïve announcements in history! I don't know whether UFOs exist or not; but I do think that it is most important to find out whether they do.

Before talking more about these UFOs, however, let me return for a moment to the report of wheels in the sky. There may be nothing more in it than coincidence. Someone, being unable to describe it in any other manner, may call a revolving object a wheel; but it is at least curious that symbols described by archaeologists as 'sun discs' are by no means rarely found carved on stones of the Megalithic and Early Bronze Ages in western Europe. Sometimes they are simply a ring; again they may be a ring with a dot in the centre and, more curiously, a ring with a

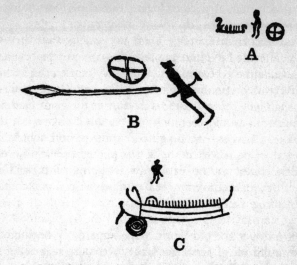

Figure 9 Wheels in the sky? So-called sun discs from
Scandinavian early Bronze Age rock engravings. A. Giant, ship
and wheel, Bohuslan, Sweden. B. Giant, spear and wheel, Stjørdal,
Norway. C. Giant, ship and wheel, Bohuslan. Similar but rougher
engravings have been found elsewhere in western Europe,
including Ireland.

cross carved upon it. A sequence of these carvings, not in-
frequently found together with symbols of ships, is published
from Brittany to Ireland and from there to the celebrated Swedish
rock engravings. A case has been made out for the existence of a
complete sequence of ship and sun disc symbols from Scandinavia
to ancient Egypt. Frequently they are so crudely executed that
without a knowledge of more perfect examples it would be impossible to interpret the pictures. But with a sequence available
there can be little doubt what was intended by the carvers. In
the most celebrated burial cairn of New Grange on the Boyne in
Ireland there is one of these symbols in the central chamber. No
one would probably have been able to identify it without a knowledge of the Swedish and Breton engravings; but with this
knowledge the intention is clear. Are these discs meant to represent the sun at all; or was the idea to picture the vehicles in which
the gods were transported through the heavens?

For many years I have just taken it for granted that when

the older generation of archaeologists talked of these things as 'sun discs', they knew what they were talking about. Now, as with so many other current dogmas, I am not so sure that they did. Even if the ancient Egyptian symbols did come to represent the Sun God, Ra, and the boat in which he daily crossed the heavens, is this what was originally intended? Was not Ra himself one of the sons of God, venerated in later years as the great God himself? Of course it would be much less trouble to leave it all unquestioned; to go on as if nothing had happened and nobody had ever reported seeing wheels in the sky, or photographed objects up there which could not be explained in terms of present day knowledge. But, if we have any real curiosity in our make up, we cannot just shrug it all off.

What we can say at this stage is that at the approximate time when men all over the old world were apparently beginning to venerate a multitude of aerial gods, they were also suggesting that they moved about the heavens in boats and things with or like wheels. Through the ages these gods took on varying characteristics, but this was doubtless due to frequent repetition and downright invention by the priestly castes, whose job it was to keep the beliefs in being. All this too was imposed apparently upon a set of earlier beliefs in which men had a tribal totem in the form of some animal. The combination of the totem animals with gods in human form who flew about the heavens produced some very curious creatures indeed.

Although I am not qualified to do so and have no real personal experience of the matter at all, I must try to make some estimate of how the problem of the UFOs strikes me as an ordinary member of the populace.

I look on it all with a completely open mind. I neither believe nor disbelieve. However I do have one article of faith and that is that a witness should be believed until he can be shown to be either lying or mistaken. The answer so often returned to a report on the supposed sightings of an UFO, that it was the planet Venus, has added to the general popular disbelief in the announcements of specialists. Next to the sun and moon Venus has always been the most well-known object in the night sky. One of the first questions asked by children when shown the darkened heavens is: 'What is that bright star?' When, in addition, the supposed specialists have on occasion claimed this well-known object to have been the cause of a report and it has been shown that the planet was not above the horizon at the time, one's doubts of the specialists' qualifications rise considerably. In fact the frequent mention of Venus and the recent statement from America that there are about seven hundred reports which they have not been able to explain, convinces me that there is a case to answer. Either there is something to hide, or the authorities are completely stupid. One remembers Bernard Shaw putting into the mouth of a foreign politician: 'For God's sake don't frighten the British.' Now it should be changed to the 'Americans'. For obviously if there are people capable of flying here frequently in large machines from outer space, they would also be advanced enough to flatten America, Russia, China and the whole caboodle had they wished to do so.

The first type of unknown objects which have been claimed as visitors from outside the earth seem to resemble the ball of light which I saw long ago at Alton. As a general rule they appear to be relatively small and to have some form of mentality in control. Known as 'foo fighters' during the Hitler war they were frequently observed following, pacing and otherwise performing evolutions round planes of all the warring nations. No one has ever explained what they are. However it has been suggested in recent years that they may be some form of animal life belonging to high levels of the earth's atmosphere, or even to outer space itself. They emit their own light and that more in the manner of a glow worm than of any artificial form. It is not thought that these objects are any kind of machine, neither do they seem to be 'witch fires', 'Will o' the wisps' or anything of that nature. They have been vouched for by very many airmen and any of these bold enough to report what they had seen were usually snubbed or told to keep quiet about it. Whatever they may be, they are not of interest in this inquiry.

The second type is completely different to the first and is the one for our consideration. It has been reported with such great frequency from all over the world that it must either be a genuine phenomenon, or some hallucinatory mental trick unknown to science. We all know 'spots before the eyes' and things of that sort; but we do not normally observe discs of enormous size racing about the skies or try to follow them in aeroplanes. Odd things do happen of course, like the well-known story of the man at a shoot who, thinking he was aiming at a flying bird, was in reality deceived by a midge on his spectacles. But you cannot photograph a bird when it is really a midge before your eyes. Yet this has frequently been done with these unknown objects.

Remember that I have never seen one of these things. I may have seen a couple of ghosts, in which about a third of the population cannot believe, but I have never seen the kind of UFO known commonly as a flying saucer and my estimate is entirely derived at second hand from the reports of others. It appears then that a very large number of people claim to have seen these flying saucers and an appreciable number have been photographed with varying success. Some of the photographs may be faked, others appear to be genuine. Looking at the photographs, usually much enlarged and therefore indistinct, one appears to see an object not at all unlike an old-fashioned humming top, cut across the middle horizontally. Only the upper part therefore is seen. The handle at the top is reduced to a spike. The reports on the size of these objects vary very much, but all agree that they are often much larger than any present day aeroplane and that they can travel at much greater speed. They can also change their course at right angles to the line of flight which no earthly plane can attempt to do.

Accounts of the lighting of these machines vary considerably. They may appear as silvery discs in daylight or glow with different colours at night. They may also, when seen fairly close at hand, appear to have a ring of windows or ports which emit bright light.

There are a fair number of reports that these machines have been observed to land and also that humanoid figures have been seen to emerge from them. It is doubtful whether any of these reports can be taken at their face value. However it seems possible that some of them may be true. I rather discount the accounts that observers have talked to persons emerging from these things and messages on the soles of shoes seem most improbable. If any conversations have taken place, which I doubt, they have not been recorded in such a way as to carry conviction. If visitors from elsewhere wished to make contact with people on earth, it does not seem probable that they would do so in American deserts or waste places in Scotland. Since they apparently can operate the machines at far greater speed than any earthly aeroplane, it would be reasonably safe for them to land openly on some civil airfield. But they have been chased, so the reports go, and apparently attacked, with dire results to the attacker.

There seems to be little doubt that these things have been picked up on radar screens and that warplanes have been sent up in pursuit; but whether this has only happened in America is not disclosed.

The term 'flying saucer' is not so inaccurate as anyone might suspect. A fair number of photographs appear to show large objects in the sky, not unlike a saucer with a rim facing downwards, but on what should be the base of the saucer there appears to be a small tower and something like a short mast. Seen from below these objects appear as discs and so we come to the description of 'wheels in the sky'.

There are many reports of these things flying in formation and in quite considerable numbers. By that I mean you might observe eight or ten at a time.

There are also reports of gigantic cylindrical mother ships on which the saucers home and into which they return. As far as I know there are no reports of such things from Britain, although there are several from France. More than one saucer is also not common in this country.

Of course all this rigmarole seems very improbable to many people and quite incomprehensible until this century. But students of the subject have noted that it is nothing new and that there are accounts at various stages of history, which could well be taken to refer to the same type of object. Pride in the achievements of modern aeronautics and conceit in the intelligence of the people on earth make it hard for most to look at all this objectively. For so long a time has humanity been taught that it is the highest product of nature that it is difficult for it now to believe that some other organism somewhere else might be more advanced. But this is not improbable at all. In fact it is more probable than not.

There are a few other significant points. For instance, it is not uncommon for it to be reported that the passing over of a saucer stops the magneto of a car, which in itself suggests some very powerful electronic device in action. Then some observers, including policemen in South Wales, have apparently observed a succession of saucers diving into the sea. They were well scolded for their pains! Other policemen on night patrol in Devon have chased apparent UFOs in fast cars and been told that they were observing planes refuelling in the air. I am sure they did not believe this explanation. Policemen have to be good observers.

There are accounts, too, of filaments of unknown substance falling from these machines and known as 'angels' tears'. No one appears to have been able to collect and examine any samples. However 'angels' tears' was the name given by German children to the fine silvery ribbons dropped by our planes during the war to deflect the German radar. I have seen plenty of these 'angels' tears', but do not know of what metal they were composed.

This is a very brief summary of what appears to be known about a very curious subject. There are a host of books available from which the reader can attempt to form his own ideas. However, I think that it must be a very dull-witted person who does not want to know the answer. Is a very large proportion of humanity suffering from delusions or are we really having visitors from outer space? If the second is the right answer, what are they coming for?

The Russians are a hard-headed and incredulous breed, but years ago they let it out that they believed they had found evidence that there had been visitors from outer space. Of course they have also announced that some of their scientists had chased what we should call a 'Loch Ness Monster' in a motor boat. This is another subject which is anathema to our orthodox zoologists. Neither account may be true. We have no means of checking them. But here is a curious point : if either the Russians or the Americans had any doubt that the things were coming from elsewhere, one would surely have accused the other of infringing their air space. Both must have been having the same kind of visitors, or hallucinations, and they know it. It is interesting too that both countries are working hard to find out the facts of extra-sensory perception or bio-electronics. They both hope to be able to talk by telepathy to people in rockets on the further side of planets which cannot be reached by radar. In our investigation then we appear to be chasing something which is cloaked in layer upon layer of official secrecy.

Seven

Although much of what has been written so far is not strictly orthodox, the present chapter is far worse and deals with matters, which are fit really only for the television plays called 'Dr Who'.

The ordinary belief of those who have convinced ideas about flying saucers is that these machines originate on Venus. The Russians of course reported that their probe showed that the atmosphere of Venus was not suitable for life, but this may not deserve complete credence, as the rocket passed a very long way from the planet. However, there is another school of thought with a far more original idea. This school believes that the visitors do not belong to our time at all; but are people living in the future who will have invented machines which are capable of coming back down the ages to see what was going on at a given time. We will now try to see whether we can conceive any possibility that this might be true. However we must note that, in the event of its being correct, there is clearly no possibility that people in flying saucers could ever have been thought of as the sons of God or have fathered children on the daughters of men. They could only have been something resembling ghosts to the people in whose ages they appeared, for they would be on a different level of vibration, with no bodily functions comparable to the people they went to investigate. At least this is how the situation would appear to me with my very limited knowledge.

To get any idea of whether such a time machine could be built, it is necessary to take a brief look at what appears to be revealed by the pendulum study of bio-electronics, ESP or psychic matters, if you prefer those terms. (However the reader is warned that the following paragraphs are rather difficult and they can be skipped if they are tedious.) It seems that every thought form, whether concrete or abstract, responds to a given rate that is a certain length on the pendulum. It is further differentiated by the number of revolutions which the pendulum makes before returning to its normal back and forth, oscillatory, form of motion. These rates range from 0 to 40 inches, which is the rate for sleep or death. By plotting these rates, it can be shown that they all lie on an Archimedian spiral curving up from 0 to 40. It can also be shown that from 0 a similar but reversed spiral curves downwards again. We are not concerned here with the complementary spiral, but only with the first one. 0 is in fact the point of birth and it appears that life proceeded before this point and also continues for several sequences of 40 beyond the point of death. Therefore it seems probable that life extends to infinity both before and behind the point of birth. We have been able to study the sex rates of fossil sea-urchins, which probably died something like two hundred millions years go.

Now, the pendulum appears to work by the repulsion of vibrations sent out by its cord when striking rays ascending or descending from the thought forms which are being investigated. Therefore everything recorded by the pendulum is in reality in reverse. This is most important when we consider time.

On the earth plane, which forms the first ascending whorl of the spiral and ends at 40, it is impossible to find a rate for time. Time on earth is always rushing away and cannot therefore be contacted. On the second whorl, that is after 40 and before 80, you can contact time on a rate of 60 inches. Knowing what we do about the reversed meaning of the rates, it is evident that time as we know it does not exist on the second whorl, which is really a mental level. Our minds, as we might call them, or souls or spirits as they would be termed by religious people, continue on the second whorl in a timeless state.

This is extremely difficult to understand, but appears to be a fact. The pendulum also shows that after 80, at the end of the second whorl, time cannot once more be contacted and therefore the timeless period ceases. However we are not concerned with this here.

As far as our research into this subject has gone, it is clear that almost every thought concept, except time, continues on the second whorl as it did on the first; green is still green and copper still copper. The second whorl then is a timeless replica of the first. Sequence is still there, but there is no time, or perhaps any time you like, between the events in the sequence.

The easiest way in which I can represent this situation is to take a sequence in our earth time as a ruler marked in numbered divisions and a sequence on the second whorl as a dot surrounded by numbered rings with no spaces between them.

It is perfectly easy to make a diagram of this but you have to leave a little space between each numbered ring in the upper sequence in order to be able to see the rings. The upper sequence on the second whorl will also not be exactly above the lower, or earth one because it is further out on the ascending spiral. There is a second difference. The earth sequence proceeds in one direction in a straight line, but the upper sequence appears as a double row of numbers both before and behind the dot which represents its origin.

Now if you draw this diagram on paper, using two parallel lines to represent the two mental levels and join the corresponding numbers in the two sequences, it is apparent that, after a certain point, events on the higher level precede the corresponding events in earth time. For this reason mediums, or sensitives as they are now called, who can jump in mind from one level to the next, can to some extent foretell the future. It will not be completely correct, because the positions of the two sequences are not exactly above one another; but it may be near enough to cause great surprise to those who listen to the medium's pronouncements.

The same appears in dreams, as was demonstrated years ago by Dunne in his *An Experiment with Time* and as we have found out by studying our own dreams and those of our friends. Although it does not concern our present study, it is interesting to notice that, if you join the numbers on the earth sequence to those behind the dot in the upper sequence, you get a reversal of the whole thing, which is often noted by people who study their dreams.

If our observations are correct, it is now reasonably clear that humanity has a second mental level, a timeless state, in which the mind can travel backwards and forwards in regard to earthly time. You can get in touch with this level in various ways and always visit it in sleep. A simple gadget, such as the pendulum, can put you in touch with this mental level. It is also clear that whatever information you can bring back to the earth level is liable to a certain distortion owing to the changes in the observer's position due to the expanding whorls of the spiral. A medium may foretell the future with surprising accuracy; but it will not always come exactly true.

An interesting sidelight on this, which also gives some indication of the probable dif.erence in rate of vibration between the two layers, is given by the reports of what is known as 'out of the body experience'. Apparently everyone leaves their body during sleep; but it is only on rare occasions that they find themselves in a position where they can observe what is happening. There is a large bulk of reports from people who have had the experience. I have had letters from several correspondents describing what they have noted, and I have talked to a parson staying here who actually found himself outside and above his body while he was taking a service. It may happen during an illness, an accident or under an anaesthetic. Many of the reports are so clear and accurate that it is obviously not a form of hallucination. The observer does apparently leave his body, regard it from about the height of six to seven feet and always find himself to one side of it.

This is explained easily when we know about the spiral of pendulum rates. We know that the spiral is climbing, but this now gives us the approximate angle of climb. It is not exact, because we do not know the exact position of the eye level of the person who is out of his body; but we can get an average, which must be fairly near the truth. The height of one body above the other is about 80 inches.

Now the pendulum rate for a person living on the earth level is 20 inches and the rate for sleep and death 40 inches. I may have made some stupid mistake, but it seems to me that in a distance of 20 inches the spiral has climbed 80 inches, a very steep climb of four in one. I am no mathematician and may easily be mistaken, but I think this means that the rate of vibration on the second mental level is four times as fast as that on earth.

Apparently everything on earth has a corresponding rate on the second level, with the exception of time of course. But since the rate of vibration is so much higher, everything has gone well beyond the earth's light spectrum. This is why you cannot normally see persons who are no longer living in their earth bodies; nor can you feel, or hear them. According to what we have learnt, however, they are still living in surroundings containing everything that we are used to on the earth level, but in a timeless state. This has an immediate bearing on our time machine problem.

If scientists could get rid of the mental block which prevents them investigating a vast subject right under their noses, they could soon learn a great deal more than my wife and I are capable of doing. The block no longer seems to restrain scientists in America and Russia. Frenchmen have been through it for years. Let us assume that in a hundred years' time the block will have gone completely and what is now known as the 'odd' will have become a commonplace of bio-electronics. By then it will be possible, no doubt, to get on to the second mental whorl at will, using some elaborate electronic machine to alter the vibrational rate.

I should imagine this would necessitate some kind of dynamo to produce a field of force around the experimenters and this would be contained in a hemispherical type of housing. Having altered your personal bio-electronic field of force from that of your earth body to the vibrations of the next whorl, you would be in the timeless zone and could go backwards and forwards in time. It would probably be possible also to move the whole machine instantly in any direction by the power of thought. This hypothetical machine is not at all unlike what is reported of the flying saucers. But there is a snag. The machine itself having gone into the second level would not be normally visible to the people on earth that the operators went to visit. It might be visible to some, who today are classed as psychics or sensitives. Their vibrational level is already somewhat higher than that of their neighbours. It is difficult too to see how the occupants of the machine could possibly get out of it to make any contact with the people they went to study. They might stop the thing in the air above some place of earth activity of another age, but, once they passed out through their artificial field of force, they would be back in their laboratory in a future time. Of course ways may be devised of getting round this difficulty; but I am unable to see far enough ahead to imagine them. I think visitors from the future could not emerge on the earth of ancient Rome or anywhere else, except in their own time.

There is much to be said in favour of this explanation of the appearance of flying saucers. Interest in the past is very widespread today and appears to be growing. It would be completely fascinating to be able to go back and see exactly what really went on in bygone ages. Should the construction of such machines become possible, they might well become subject to commercialism. You could hire a seat in a saucer to watch the building of a pyramid or the battle of Marathon. They would be of the greatest value in the study of geology and for estimating the probable changes in climate or sea level. In fact they would be of considerable importance in many ways. The way that saucers are reported as remaining stationary in the sky for hours at a time is what you would expect if a party was examining a particular place at a particular period of time. The casual way in which only some people see them while others do not suggests that they may not be visible to anybody who does not happen to have a high vibrational rate himself. In fact they are future ghosts if this explanation is correct.

We need not boggle at the word ghost. A ghost is something out of its normal earthly time sequence. All recorded television pictures are ghosts. They appear absolutely real on your television screen, but they are not there at all. Neither would this hypothetical type of unknown flying object be real in the sense that your breakfast is real. It would be something completely upsetting to what is called our 'space time continuum'. But many upsetting things are always happening nowadays, so why not this?

In one way this theory ought to be a considerable encouragement to the numerous people who work themselves into a fret through expectation of the destruction of humanity in an atomic war. If people are coming back from the future to look at us, there can have been no universal destruction before their time. Still, once again this is not necessarily correct. The visitors need not be coming from the earth plane future. They may be people living on the second plane itself and be what is in earth terms described as dead. Of course if you have a rigid belief that life is confined to one short phase on earth, there is no point in thinking about this possibility at all. But this is only a dogma and really the antithesis of any scientific outlook. You do not know the answer and your belief is on a par with that of the moon being made of blue cheese. It is known that the composition of the moon is rock and not cheese, while such evidence as there is appears to point to the conclusion that life continues to infinity. If it does, and people continue to live on a higher vibrational level on the next whorl and even on others above that, then presumably they might at times use the intelligences they had brought up with them to study the past of the level which they had left. They are not in the time sequence and not in the earth body, but it might be easier for them to lower their vibrations and even get out of their machines than people from the earth level itself. Have they ever done this? If they did, could they have had real personal contact with the earth humans they met on their trips?

I have asked a lot of difficult questions already in this book, but this one is more likely to land me in a pickle than most. All through history there have been occasional great teachers, often now spoken of by the Hindu term, 'avatar', whose births seem to have been inexplicable and teachings far higher than those of the surrounding populace. Did these avatars come down from higher levels of deliberate purpose to try to help people living on a lower level of vibration? There appear to have been female avatars as well as male; although they are not often mentioned nowadays. Aradia, the avatar of the religion now known as witchcraft, was supposedly born of the goddess, Diana, and taught her disciples both how to handle the bio-electronic power and the freedom of the individual, in a manner strongly reminiscent of the great male teachers. The only candidate that I know of from America was Quetzalcoatl, also a character of mysterious origin. It is interesting, too, that, though he did not apparently actually claim that rank, Jesus did not deny that he was a son of God. He seemed rather to imply that all or many men were this, although they did not know it. At the same time he insisted that he was the son of Man. Presumably here once again we are up against the old difficulty of the real meaning of words.

The paternity of all the avatars is mysterious. This of course may be an idea of the priestly caste to add glamour to the founder of their particular religion. Even Buddha, although claimed by the orthodox to have come from a respectable princely family, is said to have been fathered by an elephant. By this one supposes that the elephant-headed god, Ganesa, is implied. However to go into the maze of Indian mythology would be more trouble than it is worth. It is more incomprehensible to the western mind than that of ancient Greece or Rome. The point to remember about three of the avatars at any rate is that they were able to instruct their followers not only with a general code of behaviour but how to control the power of living electricity, which is apparently what ESP is. The Buddhists took this teaching to much greater lengths than anybody in the west. The Christians largely either failed to grasp it or forgot it. The witches knew a lot about it and even bred people deliberately to increase their so-called psychic powers.

The importance of this in our particular inquiry lies in the fact that anyone living on a level of what we might perhaps call 'higher potential' would have to lower his voltage in some way before being able to cope with earthly surroundings at all. He would also have to register. That means that somehow he had to make allowances for the distortion due to the position of things on the two, or perhaps more, different whorls on the spiral. It is here then I can see a possible error happening nearly two thousand years ago. In the Biblical story of the terrible future calamity in which the sun would be 'turned into darkness and the moon into blood', had there been a mistake in which ring in the sequence on the timeless level had been taken? Was Jesus really talking about something which had already happened? If it has been recorded correctly, Jesus evidently thought that it would happen in the lifetime of some of his companions.

Some of them may well have still been living at the time of Titus' siege of Jerusalem in A.D. 70, but, although this was a revolting siege according to Josephus, it was nothing to compare with the events which Jesus apparently foresaw.

I am well aware that many far more clever men than myself must have spent many hours thinking about this discrepancy and my suggestion may be offending a lot of people. Yet one must tell the truth as far as one can see it. In this particular matter there was an error, either in foretelling the future or in the recording of what was said. The great trouble, which looks like the description of an atomic war, had either happened long before or was not going to happen for perhaps two thousand years.

Eight

Of course what I have mentioned at the end of the last chapter will not fit in with the suggestion that flying saucers may be time machines, not yet made but going to be made, by people living on the earth. For one thing it seems improbable that they could ever get out of their machines without instantly returning to their own period of earth time. For another it is impossible to think of how, having got out of these machines, they could become apparently normal members of the society in which they found themselves. I do not think that the theory of future earthly time machines will work, intriguing though it is.

As far as the problem of UFOs then goes, we are left with two possibilities. They may be either contemporary visitors from some unknown planet or they may be the work of people, spoken of today as dead, living in a timeless zone above that of our own earth. The first supposition would have seemed utterly impossible before the days of H. G. Wells, but is today quite a commonplace idea. It may be difficult to guess what planet they might be coming from but no longer utterly improbable. Even with our primitive modern rockets, it is possible to see that the problems of long space travel might be overcome by any fortunate, or perhaps unfortunate, discovery in a comparatively few years.

The second idea would still seem fantastic to very many people who are still wedded to a concept of only one stage of living and that confined to the surface of a single earth. An earth with onion skins of different levels of existence cannot easily be grasped by people with a materialistic or rationalistic upbringing. Yet this idea would not seem particularly strange to advanced Buddhist or Hindu thinkers. The Buddhists with their 'wheel of life' are very near it but have not apparently as yet seen that the wheel is a double spiral. In fact, as Jesus so rightly said, you have to 'become again as little children' and reorientate all your ideas from the start. This, thanks largely to the inventiveness of television script writers, children of today appear to be quite ready to do. It means little to them that people should jump about in time and space. I have quite a number of letters from teenagers who obviously have a good idea of the possibilities, although they tell me that their views are ridiculed by their elders.

There are pointers to the occurrence of the second type of happening in the Bible itself, but since the witnesses who observed the incidents clearly did not understand what appears to have been taking place, the orthodox interpretation is not particularly convincing nowadays. You can appreciate that much of the reporting in the Bible is true without believing a word of the dogma, which has been built up upon it through the ages. That is one of the difficulties today. Because of the incredibility of the dogma, people tend to throw away the baby with the bath water.

The two incidents which we must look at both concern ascents into heaven. The first is that of Elijah and is simply a traditional story somewhat dramatized by whoever wrote it down. The second is the Ascension itself and apparently a far more accurate account. But there is a great similarity between the two stories. Not only that, but also they are very much like the dematerializations which are reported as being performed by Hindu and Buddhist sages to this day.

The Ascension is by far the most important and is entirely distinct from the vexed question of what really happened at the Crucifixion. At the Ascension a living man actually vanished in the sight of a large number of people. It is very hard to dismiss this as an account of a conjuring trick because it made such a great impression on those who saw it that it has not been forgotten for nearly two thousand years. Conjuring tricks are a commonplace in the Eastern world and had it been one no such impression would have survived. The incident carried complete conviction.

I may seem unduly credulous here, but one must remember that very little history is in any way exact. As recently as the great battle of Jutland, when I was still at school, there was only one case of exact reporting. A boy seaman in a destroyer was made to write in the log the time and the exact bearing of every incident which took place. As a reward for this devotion to duty, the boy was taken ashore afterwards and given the best meal his heart desired at the expense of the destroyer's first lieutenant. The lieutenant himself, the only man in the whole British fleet who realized the importance of a record, received no commendation at all, although he eventually retired from the Navy as a captain.

I have spent much of my life trying to interpret history from scraps of archaeological information and snippets from ancient chronicles, clearly written down long after the events which they purported to record. I am perhaps then in a position to form some kind of estimate of the type of record which we can all read in the Gospels. As far as I can judge, this is quite as good and probably better than anything recorded in classical, or medieval history. It is perhaps about as reliable as what can be learnt of Wellington's campaign in the Peninsula, but far more exact than say what has been told of the Black Prince's campaign which ended at Poitiers. Compared with what little has survived of the history of William the Conqueror's campaigns and adventures, it is as accurate as modern journalism. Of course this is only my view and anyone who likes may dispute it. I am neither anti-clerical, nor pro-clerical. I simply wish to find things out.

Having said this much, let us see what the Gospels appear to relate. I have taken the two following accounts from J. B. Phillips' recent translation of the Gospels, but they are little different from the wording of the James I version :

> Then He led them outside as far as Bethany, where He blessed them with uplifted hands. While He was in the act of blessing them He was parted from them and was carried up to Heaven. (St Luke)
> When He had said these words He was lifted up before their eyes till a cloud hid Him from their sight. (St John)

It is clear, I think, that the witnesses did not understand what had happened and the words 'carried up to Heaven' and 'a cloud hid Him from their sight' were added to the straightforward report in explanation of an apparently impossible event. However, if we remember the numerous reports of 'out of the body' experiences and the evidence of the spiral, it is possible to see what had happened. Jesus, a master of bio-electronic power, had simply accelerated his vibrations and moved up on to the next whorl of the spiral. There, as we have already observed, he would be invisible to the watchers. There are numerous modern Hindu accounts of this feat being performed by their learned men and also of their subsequent return. The whole Ascension story in the Gospels is claimed as the promise of human survival of death and, as far as one can judge, indeed it is, but hardly of the type of survival which is generally imagined. This is in itself a glorified picture of what was believed to be the most happy situation two thousand years ago. The harps and songs and all the rest of it are a reflection of that bygone age, when a feast was the height of enjoyment.

The Elijah story may well have once been similar. In fact some Hindu experts believe Jesus to have been a reincarnation, not of Elijah but of his disciple Elisha, who was promised a double portion of Elijah's spirit if he could see him carried into heaven. The point about Elijah's aerial exploit is that it has been quoted in various works as evidence for the former existence of flying saucers. What actually does the Bible say?

... Elijah said unto Elisha, Ask what shall I do for thee, before I be taken away from thee. And Elisha said, I pray thee, let a double portion of thy spirit be upon me.

And he said, Thou hast asked a hard thing : nevertheless, if thou see me when I am taken from thee, it shall be unto thee; but if not, it shall not be so.

And it came to pass, as they still went on, and talked, that, behold, there appeared a chariot of fire, and horses of fire, and parted them both asunder; and Elijah went up by a whirlwind into heaven.

And Elisha saw it, and he cried, My father, my father, the chariot of Israel and the horsemen thereof. And he saw him no more ... (Authorized Version. 2 Kings, 2, verses 9–11)

This dramatic story had probably been handed down by word of mouth for a long time before it was put into writing. The vehicle, if there was one, was indescribable and so spoken of as a chariot. A chariot had to have horses and they were added, quite reasonably. But nobody emerged from the chariot; although

Elijah apparently knew it was coming. When it came he vanished in a whirlwind.

One can see how this story fits in well with modern accounts of flying saucers; but we are left with a doubt whether anything more than a dust-devil, or willy-waw, was ever seen. Elijah, an accomplished practitioner of ESP (or shall we call it magic?) simply vanished. How he went nobody probably, not even Elisha, ever knew. I don't know how it strikes others, but I personally suspect that Elisha had to say he had seen the chariot to explain his subsequent magic powers. One wonders too whether the scribe who wrote this story down was familiar with the Greek beliefs in which gods flew about the heavens in chariots drawn by horses.

Whatever may have been the truth of Elijah's disappearance, and the story as told would not be out of place in the Arabian Nights, a feeling remains that it may have been very like the Ascension. Unfortunately there was only a single witness and there is quite a possibility either that he may have been biased in his subsequent account, or that the author of the second book of Kings was somewhat carried away by the drama of the incident. On the whole it does not seem possible to use this story as an argument in favour of the former existence of flying saucers.

When we turn to the problem of how anyone could possibly pass from one level of vibration to one of a perhaps four times faster rate, we are humbugged by a lack of general knowledge. It is a problem well ahead of science at its present stage. We do know that a living scientist today is not the solid object he appears to be, but is really almost entirely empty space, a series of holes joined together by French knitting. In fact he may only be there at all because somebody else thinks of him. In any case you could have dozens of different scientists fitted into the holes in the first one.

People used to think that they knew all about matter; but today they do at least realize that they hardly know anything at all. Matter may be energy, still what is that? Energy may be vibrations. What are they? All that is really known is that if you do certain things, certain results will follow and the range of action in which the foreseeable results are known is very limited. It has not even begun to dawn on the scientific world that, by changing the rate of vibration, you might land bang in another scientific world much more advanced than your own.

The Hindu and Buddhist thought looks at all this in a different way. It believes that, after training your mind very severely for a long time, you are able to change the composition of your body, transport it instantly to somewhere else and appear there in the form in which you started. You can then return at will. This action, known as dematerialization, is so foreign to orthodox western science that its possibility is only envisaged in books of imagination and on the television screen. But there are people who practise leaving their bodies at will.

We had, some years ago, one of these people living at Hole Mill down the hill below us here. She told us that she used to leave her body at night and go into her friends' houses to see how they were getting on. Naturally, owing to our early training, we did not take these statements seriously. Something, however, happened which made us wonder whether we had been entirely wrong.

One day I was busy on a bit of walling in the garden, when this friend, who had spent long years in the study of magic, came up and began to talk about it. While working, I listened as she described how she protected her house from visits by people she did not want to see. She constructed a pentagram in her mind and put it on her gate. If she wished to rid a house of an unpleasant atmosphere, she reversed the pentagram. That night, before I went to sleep, I practised making mental pentagrams round our beds as an exercise to see if I could draw such things in my mind. I went to sleep and thought no more about it.

Some nights later my wife woke in the dark, feeling that somebody was in the room. She saw a faint glow of light moving round the ends of the beds and on to the wall. It vanished and that was all. The feeling of someone's presence went also.

We did not see the friend for about a fortnight and then she dropped in for tea. In the course of conversation, she asked : 'Has somebody been putting protection on you?' 'Not that I know of,' I answered. 'Why do you ask?' 'Well,' she said, 'I came into your bedroom the other night to see if you were all right and I could not get near the bed because of the triangles of fire round it.'

This story was inexplicable by any ordinary means. How could she have known about my pentagram exercise and why should my wife have felt the presence, and seen the moving light? But the Hindus and Buddhists state that, when dematerialized, they can be seen as small, moving balls of light.

Since that time I have frequently tried the pentagram exercise and taught other people how to do it. We have had people, who we did not want to see, getting as far as the first pentagram and then turning round, because they felt they did not want to go on. Others who persisted got lost or ditched their cars. Although I still cannot believe that my pentagrams had this effect, I can only report what happened and say that I am sufficiently super-stitious to renew the pentagrams at intervals in the hope of dis-couraging unwelcome guests.

This is all very strange to properly brought up people. I do not really believe in it; yet when people ask me how to get rid of an unwanted lover, or a nasty smell in the night, I tell them to try a pentagram. On three occasions I have been told that it worked. It seems to me that the actual pentagrams have nothing to do with it; they are only symbols concentrating the power of thought, that 'mana' perhaps which we met earlier on in the book. Yet if you can do such things with very little trouble by simply thinking up a geometrical figure, what could you not do if you really concentrated for years on training your thought?

Summing this up, I think that there is reasonable evidence that in Biblical times, as at the present day, certain people, perhaps after long training, could detach themselves from one level of existence and move on to another. Those of today, who either voluntarily or involuntarily do this, often affirm that they remain attached by an indefinitely extensible cord to their earthly body. This cord is apparently mentioned in the Bible ('or ever the silver cord be loosed'). If it is loosed of course the individual remains permanently on the higher level and is unable to return to his earth body. I have had letters from people who have found them-selves out of their bodies during sleep and been thrown into a panic lest the cord should be parted and they would not be able to return.

This moving between two levels of existence, however, does not seem to demand any vehicle of transport. Our lady magician, who claimed to visit us in the night, also stated that she often talked with people living on the higher level. I asked her one day to see whether she could find out from her friends what flying saucers were. A few days later she returned with the answer:

'They told me that they were made by the back-room boys. I asked them why and they said it was because it was the kind of thing that back-room boys liked to do.' I have no idea what degree of reliance to put on this statement. But if, by any chance, the saucers were mechanical toys of experimenters on another level, it would explain why only certain people see them. There is no reason to suppose that men's mentality would change after reaching the next level. Since everything else, but time, appears to be there, people with a mechanical bent might well experiment in many ways and only those with a certain degree of psychic ability on this earth level would be able to see the results. If nothing more definite is learnt about these saucers in the next few years, this answer may well be the correct one. It is a sobering thought in this self-styled technological age, but how many of the brilliant inventions on the earth level were not in reality produced by the back-room boys on the next one and then handed to the supposed earth inventors in sleep? At the beginning of wireless telegraphy the celebrated inventor, Marconi, is said to have stated at an inquiry that he had no idea how the thing worked. Others may not have been so honest.

If what I have just written is at all correct, it is difficult to see that any of the suppositions made earlier on about the prehistoric stone circles and alignments would have any value. Then we are left again with the puzzle of why prehistoric and later people should wish to charge stones and trees with bio-electronic power. This can hardly have been done just for the fun of it. Stone was evidently the most desirable substance, but in stoneless areas, timber circles were put up instead. Laws against the worship of stones and trees continued to be made far into Christian Saxon times. Why was it done?

Of course the general answer always has been 'to worship the spirit of the stone or tree'. But does this make any sense? Why quarry a stone and drag it for a great distance, simply to worship its hypothetical spirit? Why cut down a great tree and set it up in a ring with others, to worship its spirit, when you could do so much more realistically when the tree was growing? This cannot be the right answer, nor anywhere near it. In fact in many ways I prefer our first hypothesis that these things may have been set up as the equivalent of radar beacons for aerial navigation. Yet we seem to have been steadily demolishing the possibility that anyone could have used them for this purpose and many people will think that the very idea of it is completely absurd.

Shall we go back to the second question at the beginning of this book, since we appear to have reached an impasse with the first one : what was the war in heaven ?

Nine

I do not think that there would have been any possibility of guessing what the war in heaven might have been before the landing of the first man on the moon and the photographs taken of the surface of Mars. Before that time everyone had been happy in thinking that the moon had been pock-marked all over by a vast shower of meteorites, and Mars might be covered with a network of canals. Now it is known that both are pock-marked in a similar way and much of the dust of the moon is composed of tiny globules of fused glass.

Early in the Hitler war I spent a long time trying to find out why large numbers of German bombs fell in the fields within a few miles of Cambridge. There seemed to be no sense in it. I must have looked at hundreds of bomb craters and put them on a map, in order that in later years, when they had become weathered and obscured by soil, archaeologists might not be mistaken into digging them up as Bronze Age burials. I am really quite knowledgeable about what happens when bombs fall in the fields and explode at varying depths.

Most meteorites falling into Earth's atmosphere are burnt up by the friction and very little remains to land on the earth. Nobody really knows what happens when a really large one strikes the earth. Some great object fell in remote Siberia years ago, flattening and burning trees over a very wide area; but it was a very long time before anyone managed to find out where it had fallen and nobody saw it fall. Presumably this was a meteor, but its effect does not seem to have been much like the craters on the moon. Earth is not covered with hundreds of gigantic craters and the weathering of the years would not have hidden them from the inquisitive eyes of geologists. A very few in Africa have recently attracted attention. However, clearly Earth was not bombarded in any way like the same degree as the moon or Mars.

Of course I am not an astronomer, but I was trained in geology and I have been in places where craters might have been expected to survive, that is in the Arctic where there is little or no soil to obscure such things. I think it is fair to say that Earth

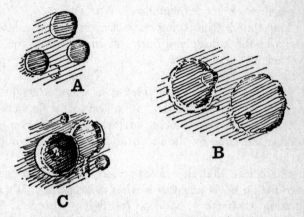

Figure 10 Rough sketches of craters on the moon, from photographs, all to one scale. It is hard to see how these could have been formed by the impact of spherical bodies falling by gravitation on to the moon's surface; but less difficult to imagine that they had been caused by huge explosions at various depths and at different times. This is most noticeable in the flattened floors of the craters shown at B. At the time when the meteor explanation was suggested, no one on earth had envisaged fission explosives or huge rockets.

was never bombarded to anything like the extent of the moon or Mars. Why not? The bombardment of the moon certainly took a considerable time, for craters overlap in a way which shows that some had been there well before others arrived. They are also all over the moon, which must have revolved while all this was going on. Of course it is possible that, although the moon was circling Earth during this time, and Mars was continuing on its orbit, Earth might have missed the bulk of the shower of meteorites. Yet surely this is most improbable. The moon had to go round Earth and yet was hit all over its surface; while Earth was hardly, if at all, touched. Mars also was apparently plastered. Does this make astronomical sense? Possible it may be, but surely the chances of it happening like that are very remote?

The moon has little or no atmosphere and is covered with dust composed of tiny globules of fused glass, which must be melted dust. There are craters of all sizes all over it and these look remarkably like the relatively tiny craters of the Hitler war. Could this possibly be the explanation? Was the moon bombarded for a long time by something resembling rockets with atomic war heads; was the atmosphere burnt off in the blasts and the dust converted into globules of glass by the heat of the explosions? Did the same thing happen to Mars? Today this is a wild guess and presumably nobody will give it a second thought. Still, if there was a war in heaven, an all-out struggle between the planets, have we been looking at the traces of it ever since we focused a telescope on the moon and looked with some awe at the craters?

I said before that this investigation was likely to get like a science fiction novel and this is what is happening. We may not be getting satisfactory evidence for flying saucers at an early time, but may we perhaps be getting suggestions that vehicles, resembling more efficient rocket capsules, may have been circling Earth a long time ago and looking for places to land? Is it not possible that the war in heaven may have been a fight between two planets as to which of them should colonize Earth?

Let us, for our amusement, and not with any sense of conviction, try to draw a picture. A very long time ago, somewhere about 2500 B.C. perhaps, there were two planets in the solar system rather more advanced technologically than Earth is today. One was Mars, the other perhaps Venus. Both of them were nearing the end of their easily obtainable mineral deposits. They communicated one with the other, yet suffered from the human failing of jealousy. In fact the people of Mars at any rate were human. Both had their eyes on Outer Space; but Mars was first in the field and occupied the moon, which at that time had more atmosphere. However owing to gravitational and other problems it was decided to build bases on it very deep underground. But the moon was only a staging post to a much bigger prize. This was Earth itself.

The inhabitants of Earth were still very primitive. They were hunters, fishermen and herdsmen. In some places small villages were perhaps slowly developing into towns; but the people were no less human than those of Mars itself. Actually a good deal is really known about the cultural accomplishments of the Earth people. We know about their stone axes and arrow heads, their coarse pottery and simple houses, their dugout canoes and their primitive ploughs. We even have a good idea what many of those in north-western Europe looked like. They were slightly built men and women with oval faces and long heads. They probably had black hair and brown eyes. There are plenty of people of this kind still living in Europe today. You can see them every time you go to London. There was not much difference in their appearance, except perhaps in the colour of their skins, right across to India and beyond. They were not more quarrelsome than men usually are and in fact neither particularly murderous, nor warlike. We speak of them in a general way today as Neolithic.

Mars, we have supposed, had by now set up its bases inside the crust of the moon. It began to dispatch rockets carrying parties of explorers and prospectors to earth. Of course the term 'rocket' is a complete guess and may be very far from the truth. The atmosphere and conditions on Earth turned out to be very similar to those on their own planet. The main objective was at first mineral deposits, but as the Neolithic people had no knowledge of metal working, the Martians had to find it all out for themselves. They were so relatively advanced as to seem superhuman to the Earth men. There was no difficulty in persuading these to work for the Martians. They probably gave them occasional delectable things to eat and bribed them in various ways to work for them. Probably the stores carried in each Martian vehicle were strictly limited and an expedition did not remain very long on Earth. There may well also have been an idea of medical experts at home that it was unhealthy to stay here for more than a few weeks.

It was during this period of exploration that the Earth natives were persuaded to set up rings of stones and timber circles to act as guiding beacons for the use of incoming space-craft. All round western Europe from Sardinia to Scandinavia teams were at work and beacons were set up. Perhaps farther east other ways of directing air traffic were devised.

For a relatively short time this reasonably happy state of affairs continued and then the jealousy of the other planet flared up into open war. Probably it also claimed Earth as its private possession.

The first campaign in the war centred on the destruction of the Martian moon bases. These were so deep underground that explosives of gigantic power had eventually to be used to get at them. Then there was a slogging match between the two planets themselves. As a result of this, Mars was knocked out and the other planet so badly disabled that it has as yet been unable to take advantage of its victory.

But the interest of all this is in what happened to the exploring parties marooned on Earth by the destruction of the bases on the moon. There was little they could do and after a very short time the Martians had to go native. In the hope, however, that relief expeditions would eventually be sent to fetch them home, they persuaded the real natives to keep up their wild dances at the stone circles and so on as a religious rite pleasing to the Great Ones in the sky, who had sent them down to live among them and bring them marvellous benefits.

This is a fairy story. I have made it up. But it is curious how it might be true. So much that happened in later history seems to add to the probability. Let us see what might have happened to the Martians. Remembering that I have been on three Arctic expeditions myself, it is possible that I might have some idea how it all might develop. We will continue our fairy story with some groups of isolated men and perhaps women too, dotted about on the surface of an undeveloped and foreign planet with little hope of ever returning home again; being shipwrecked on a desert island would be far less drastic.

These stranded astronauts would all be specialists in some way or another. If we may judge from modern trends in education, they might be deplorably lacking in simple general knowledge; but some of them surely must have known something about growing things in gardens. This was to be vital in their predicament and may well explain why such and such a god is responsible in tradition for teaching a particular people agriculture.

Botanists among them would recognize what plants might possibly provide them with grain and would institute an immediate search in the particular part of the world in which they had been stranded. A little was probably known by the natives already. Much the same thing was likely to happen in the case of metals. There would be men among them skilled in the identification of metallic ores; but there was no fuel to provide great heat for smelting. Metal for tools was an urgent necessity and copper available in many localities. Thus such and such a god became the Smith of the Gods, by teaching the natives how to make simple cupellation hearths. It is interesting to remember in this connection that the earliest metal tools, in Europe at any rate, were made of pure copper and only later was tin added to it to make the more satisfactory bronze.

There was little else they could do to better their situation. All the mechanical civilization in which they had been brought up vanished with the failure of their fuel supplies. It was useless to try to build a boat, as many men have done on the loss of their ship, to take them home again, for their home was far away across the heavens and only a relief expedition could take them back. But to the natives, to whom they had miraculously appeared from the sky, they were still wonderful. For a while they may well have still retained some ammunition for firearms of some kind and from this the stories of the power of the gods to strike a man dead in an instant could well have arisen. So too could the idea of Zeus' thunderbolts have originated in some kind of hand grenade.

As time went on in their isolation from normal life, 'the sons of God saw the daughters of men that they were fair; and they took them wives of all which they chose'. Isn't this exactly what was bound to happen? In our story too, we must assume that this took place not at the base of one lost expedition, but at several. The exploration parties were often cut off from one another by hundreds or thousands of miles of sea or impassable forest. The world they had come to was young, with none of the roads, towns or vehicles of civilization. Of necessity they must have taken to the sea, in the hope of joining up with others of their kind.

Thus, we may think, there slowly arose on Earth little tribes of hybrids with a greater knowledge than others in the world at the time. Unlike the rest, they knew how to provide a subsistence from agriculture, they knew how to make metal tools and they learnt how to use the sea. But the leaders in each group proudly claimed descent from their forefathers, who had come from the sky. Although this blood was slowly diluted by admixture with the natives; yet when possible they intermarried with those of their own kind and, throughout the old world at any rate, they became the ruling caste. How much was handed down by word of mouth of the remembered lore of the lost planet is anybody's guess. Scraps of the knowledge of how to handle bio-electronic power apparently spread to every corner of the globe and large sections of more detailed information remained in such doctrines as that of the Kahunas in the Pacific.

The most colourful traditional picture of all this fairy tale is undoubtedly that which survives from ancient Greece. Here the myths and legends are just the kind of thing which one might have expected to be found circulating hundreds of years after the astonishing and little understood happenings; but, even in the old Celtic stories, there seem to be traces of similar ideas. There we find cauldrons which revive dead men, magic spears, inexhaustible sources of food and such like things which, although clearly imaginary in their context, yet might be reflections of older events of a more concrete nature. Right down into the Viking Age, men still wore coats in battle on which swords would not bite and carried unbeatable weapons.

But if anything remotely like our fairy story should ever have happened, it appears to have been a mixed blessing. Did we not guess that the strangers came from Mars and was not Mars the planet of war? Why was it thought to be so, unless there was some vague tradition at the back of the idea? With the coming of metal, not only were improved tools for peaceful uses made available, but the weapons of war were rendered far more efficient. 'I beheld Satan as lightning fallen from heaven.' War between group and group and tribe and tribe became endemic. The greed which had wrecked the original planets seemed to have come down to earth.

We have seen that such peoples as the Aryans in India were most particular in not permitting mixed marriages with the conquered peoples. This idea was perpetuated all over the old world. In Europe in the middle ages, the regulation of marriages resembled that of the breeding of race horses today. To some extent then, the differences between the newcomers and the indigenous population were deliberately perpetuated by a hybrid caste. Of course human nature being what it is, and despite the continual struggle of the church to prevent it, there were unending lapses from strict decorum on the part of youth. The blood was continually being mixed, and Martian traits might pop up anywhere in the populace. Still, granted the first fairy tale possibility, the equality of man must be a mirage, for there would be at least two different kinds of man; the one with Martian blood and the one without it. How does this fit in with what we appear to know about humanity? Surely it fits pretty well. There are always two kinds of men, the leaders and the led: the ones who are always striving to get something done and the others who cannot be bothered even to think for themselves, as long as they are fed and amused. The assumed blood relationship of every man to every other would no longer exist, for it was only a comparatively short time since the gods came down to earth. In actual circumstances it is most doubtful whether any of our modern egalitarian enthusiasts can really believe that they are the blood brothers of the aborigines of New Guinea. A few may have swallowed this idea, but most of them have never really thought about it.

However it is extraordinary what can be done by selective breeding. A rough and clumsy wild pony can be built up by stages into a Derby winner and the process has been shown to be reversible. In fact the animal side of humanity can be changed; but nobody knows what can be done to the mental side. If you bred for thousands of years to produce ruling warriors, it could be done. If you bred for psychic potentials, as the witches did, it would work. There was perhaps no need for anything external at all to account for the situation as we now see it. The facts are that the warrior caste did breed together. Their rulers exchanged daughters from western Europe to China and southwards to northern Africa. It was bound to produce a stabilized type. However this only holds good as long as you disregard the two sides of human nature; the mental and the physical. If you regard man as entirely animal, you may perhaps be correct in thinking that, against his own wishes, you could breed him into the 'average' man and use him in a manner that a computer could decide. This is the ambition of the advocate of the human ants' nest.

But there is the other side of man which appears to stem from something outside his animal body. He can get away from this body, either in sleep or in death. This mental side of man will never admit that he is the same as any other man. After being pushed to a certain point, he will defend his belief with his life and here lies the danger which many of us see approaching today. The egalitarian idea if pushed too far is bound to end in world wide civil war. Will the people who lead this strife be in reality men of Martian ancestry?

Ten

Taking up the thread of our fairy story once again, what was likely to happen in after ages to the children of the original mixed marriages? How would they think of and describe their ancestry?

I have seen the small Eskimo tribe of the Polar Eskimoes, near what is now called Thule in north-west Greenland. This group of cheerful, little, copper-coloured men and women had two remarkable men among them. One was the natural son of Peary the American explorer and the other that of a negro, whom he took on his expedition to the North Pole. These two men had more originality than the pure-bred Eskimo and became natural leaders. I never saw the men in question, but was told about them when I was up there in 1937. Peary apparently took a considerable interest in Eskimo women and one of his books is full of nude photographs. There is no accounting for taste and no women of known race are unattractive to some men of another. Actually there are many half-caste Greenlanders and I have seen French sailors in Godhavn hunting for Eskimo girls like terriers after rats.

It would seem that, among the northern Eskimoes at any rate, a mixed-breed tended to become a leader, not only in cases I have mentioned but in several communities further to the south. He was not indeed a son of a god, but of someone born of people with a far more elaborate culture.

In other parts of the world, especially in those where the two cultures are not of very different levels, the situation is reversed and half-breeds are often regarded as a disgrace by one people or both. A well-bred Chinese deplored the marriage of his daughter to a European and what used to be called a Eurasian was not thought fit to mix with white society.

In the Near East and in India, relatively high civilizations tended to be overrun and conquered by far more barbarous but more warlike races. The Aryans, at first the less cultured people, would not intermarry at all with those they had subdued. As a general rule, it seems that the peoples in antiquity were named by their neighbours. In Ptolemy's *Geography*, for instance, we find a tribe in Galloway simply called Novantes, the New Comers, by the Romans and probably Cruithnigh by their neighbours. Others were named Cats of War or Cow People according, one imagines, to their totems. Therefore when you find the sons of God, it seems probable that other people called them that. These other people would hardly have applied such a term to barbarian invaders. Whoever the sons of God were, they must surely have been of a much higher culture than those who gave them the name.

Of course there are strange tribal names like the Gold Guarding Gryphons mentioned by Herodotus, who were presumably some mongoloid tribe in Central Asia with distinctive head-dresses; but, as far as one can see, it is most improbable that any people in those far-off times had the pride to call themselves 'the sons of God', and it is unlikely that any other people gave them such a grandiloquent title. However it could be the name of a distinctive breed which cropped up among a variety of peoples, like perhaps the way in which we speak of an 'Arab' stallion. Old men and women might nod their heads when looking at a child and remark, 'One of the sons of God'. 'Ah, yes, you can see it in the eyes', or something of that kind.

I myself have heard a Cornishman, a tall, dark man with a beaked nose and yellow eyes, described as 'one of those Phoenicians'. This may have been the result of modern education. It is well over two thousand years since the Phoenicians are believed to have mined tin in Cornwall. If this was a genuine piece of Cornish folk lore, it gives us a good yardstick for judging how long such ideas might persist.

If it comes to that, I have also heard a crofter in South Uist telling a man from Skye that, 'Of course we came from Spain'. Once again this may have been a piece of Victorian education; but it could well have been a genuine tradition and quite possibly correct. It surprised me when I heard it, out in Kilpheder sand dunes, with the Atlantic roaring on the long sandy shore. You would not have expected the two old men to have talked about anything of the sort; but rather how the lobster fishing was going, or whether the herring had come in yet.

These things do last in a surprising way. About four years ago two brothers from Beer, some two miles away over the hill, married two girls from Branscombe. The older Branscombe men, the real natives, were shocked. It is not right to marry people from Beer they told me. I asked why not and found that the older inhabitants of Beer were thought to be black and to talk a different dialect. However it was perfectly in order to marry people from Seaton beyond Beer who did not have these peculiarities.

Actually the people of Beer seem to be no darker in skin than those of Branscombe. However I must admit that I am quite unable to understand their dialect. From childhood I have been familiar with most of the varieties in Devon, Somerset and Cornwall, but the speech of Beer is like none of them. There are vague stories of men coming ashore in boats from wrecks and this may be the answer. Still, whatever the reason may be, in 1965 men in Branscombe thought it wrong that daughters of the village should marry men from the next one. This is in our so-called technological England. What things were like in the deeply wooded, boggy, primitive Albion four thousand and more years ago we can scarcely imagine at all.

Some years before the Hitler war there was a small expedition, mostly of Cambridge men, on the east coast of Greenland. One of the members was of very fine physique and tall with it. He was approached by the elders of the local Eskimoes with a strange request which embarrassed him very much, for he was shy by nature. The elders wanted him to father a child on a young girl called Snow Bunting, in order to improve the size of their breed. Although daunting to the man in question, this caused considerable amusement to the other members of the expedition and was greeted with great delight in Cambridge some months later. Snow Bunting became a kind of password. A mention of the name to the man himself could easily have led to murder.

Although rather ridiculous today, this story surely explains a most prevalent custom in antiquity. Readers of myths and legends must have observed how in them a hero frequently arrives from a foreign land, marries the daughter of the local king and then succeeds to the throne. Known as exogamy to anthropologists, this was a custom which compelled a man to marry outside his own tribe; but in the cases we are talking about it was coupled with another, that is matriarchy, in which the mother is head of the tribe and descent is reckoned through the female line. Owing to this custom, the king is only ruler because he is married to the rightful queen. When you combine exogamy with matriarchy, it is clear that the young prince of one reigning family was compelled to go out and seek his future kingdom at the hand of the senior princess of another state. The custom still persists in parts of Africa to this day.

In our own land the last tribes to retain this custom were the Highland Picts. When the Scots from Ireland managed to get control, originally through this custom, they managed to establish patriarchy, the rule descending from father to son. This led to incessant civil wars, because claimants to the throne were always ready to make a bid for it, since they had married the rightful princess by the Pictish reckoning. The last attempt was not so many years before the conquest of England by the Normans, somewhere about the year A.D. 1000.

The distinction between patriarchy and matriarchy led to endless war and trouble all over the western world. The Romans, who had been under the first for generations, evidently could not understand what was happening in southern Britain when they found two great tribes, the Iceni of East Anglia and the Brigantes further north, in process of changing over from one form of rule to the other. Prasutagus, king of the Iceni, tried to get round the difficulty by a trick. On his death he left the kingdom to Rome. But the officers sent to stabilize this arrangement behaved with great stupidity. When the rightful queen Boudicca (Boadicea) objected, they scourged her and, what was worse, they violated her daughters, the future bearers of the sacred royal line. The result was not unexpectedly a furious rising, which led among other things to the destruction of a whole legion, one of the rarest occurrences in the whole of the history of the Roman army. Two legions were once destroyed in an ambush in the German forests, but otherwise I do not think that a single legion was ever lost in Europe.

Boudicca's revenge was to sacrifice her female captives with revolting cruelty to a moon goddess. Evidently it was believed that only by sexual atrocity could the stain on the sacred female line be wiped out.

Much the same thing happened with the Brigantes. Here the queen Cartismandua wished to change her husband Vernutius for his standard bearer. It was probably her right to change her husband for another after a regular period of years. Ordinarily, if we see what happened, for instance, in the Greek lands, Vernutius would probably have been sacrificed. But Vernutius was 'a master of war' and objected to this fate. He managed to turn Cartismandua out. She fled to the Romans and they, remembering what had happened over Boudicca, supported her. This involved them in a long war and the eventual annexation of Brigantia.

If this kind of thing happened in Britain nearly two thousand years ago, it must have happened in many other lands also. There must have been a similar but possibly more intense and secret struggle than that which attempted to restore the Stuart kings in England. This only began to fade away after the defeat of the rising of the '45'. But why were these female lines so important? Is it possible that there was some truth in our fairy story after all? Were the original mother figures the women whom the sons of God took as wives? It does not appear utterly absurd that they might have been. If they were, then the term 'son of God' might have remained in common and perhaps secret parlance far down the ages. Suppose Snow Bunting really had had a half-European baby, might not its descendants in an isolated community have preserved some memory in rather romantic terms? Of course this happened at a time when contact with European and American expeditions was becoming common and education was being spread. But it might have happened in the Elizabethan days of Henry Hudson. Then might not the father perhaps have appeared as a god from the sea—somebody coming ashore in shining armour from a great vessel whose like had never been seen before. If then men appeared from the sky in Cornwall or Spain in the dim ages more than four thousand years ago, would they not have appeared still more godlike to the stone-using inhabitants of those countries?

The whole of the fairy story is, of course, quite improbable.

None of it need have happened at all in the way in which I put it together. Furthermore, even supposing that there were these expeditions from another planet, there is nothing really to show that their personnel did not all return safely home, whether that home was subsequently destroyed or not. However, if there were visitors of this kind, then the assumption to be drawn from the brief Biblical accounts is that they were somewhat larger than the natives. Their descendants were warriors and giants. The giant form (Eskimoes are very small compared with Europeans) was what the elders wished to obtain in the case of Snow Bunting. I have been too credulous perhaps the whole way through this investigation and nothing at all may have happened, except some rather taller race, with a higher culture, overran another, presumably an early Semitic one. That is the sensible conservative way to look at it and apparently the view which the Roman Catholic priests are expected to offer if anyone should bother to ask about it.

But I am not convinced about this. Somehow it all seems rather too much for the imagination of the early Semitic, Indian and Greek peoples. We know the kind of thing which is imagined by so-called primitive folk : 'You must not swim in the sea, or a little worm will swim up inside you and you will have a baby.' Of course, you would not get anything quite so simple from people who watched and hunted wild beasts for their food, or kept them in domesticity for the same purpose. Yet even the hunters on the hill, however much they watched the soaring of the great birds of prey, would surely not have imagined easily gods who flew about the heavens and resembled themselves so closely; while the agriculturalists hardly bothered themselves with the sky at all, except to watch for the signs of coming wind and rain.

In the years following the Kaiser's war there was a story circulating which was probably apocryphal. It dealt with a supposed incident in the reign of George V when England was just as snobbish as it is today, but perhaps rather more civilized. One evening a small and rather battered vessel sailed into a famous yachting centre. She ran on up the harbour and rounded to in an area under the windows of the grand local yacht club. This club considered that this part of the harbour had been reserved for their own use by the grace of the Almighty. The little visitor let go her anchor and soon the smoke of cooking began to rise from the 'charlie-noble' of her galley. The boat's owner evidently intended to spend the night in these sacred waters.

Since some neighbouring yacht clubs were on visiting terms and were welcomed in the club's berths, the secretary studied the stained and tattered burgee flying from the offending vessel's mast head. He could not read the letters on it. Therefore he had himself pulled out to her in a boat and hailed her imperiously. No notice was taken of his hail. He was pulled alongside and scrambled up on to her deck.

From this coign of vantage the secretary peered down through the smoke pouring up through the companion-way hatch and could see a figure in a torn and dirty sweater happily engaged in frying sausages and chops over his galley fire. 'What, sir, are the letters on your burgee?' the secretary shouted down. The stranger took a pipe slowly out of his mouth and grunted 'MOBYC'.

'And what yacht club might that be?' called the secretary again. 'My Own Bloody Yacht Club,' came back the unhurried answer.

Well, my sympathies are entirely with the stranger. Frequently, after a long hammering outside, I have at last made harbour, hoping for peace and a quiet night, only to find every available berth filled by smart yachts whose shining paint and spotless decks clearly showed that their owners had never had to struggle against the sea in their lives. What I am going to write now is just as unconventional as the behaviour of that nameless mariner. The only person in all history, who seems to have claimed to be a Son of God was Jesus and He also called Himself the Son of Man. It is not clear from what is reported in the Gospel stories that the Father was the same as the creator of the universe. This is an assumption made at some time in the Dark Ages and it may well be incorrect. It is not clear either that the Father whom Jesus spoke about as His own was the same entity as the one He told His disciples that they possessed in Heaven. Yet it is on these points that the bulk of the dogma of the church today is based. Even the breach between the Greek and Roman churches turned on whether Jesus was exactly equal to His Father or slightly subordinate.

As we have seen already, the meaning of the word God varied greatly in classical times and probably only among the orthodox Hebrews did it refer to the sole creator of the universe. Although it is implied in the teaching of Jesus that all men had a father on a higher level, there seems to be nothing to draw each man's father into the single entity of the creator. In fact to me it seems much more probable that the references are to entities described by spiritualists as group souls (greater entities further up the spiral than single human minds). The whole lot may well stem in turn from the creator, but are in no way equal. Jesus appears to have been given a job to do by His group soul. Nobody really understood what He was talking about and so, on the analogy of Hebrew belief, a religion was built up which had little to do with the original intention. This in no way detracts from the value of the whole matter. Jesus did demonstrate that there was a life after death. He did show how bio-electronic power could be controlled and used for healing and other purposes and He did, I think, show quite clearly that everybody had a controlling entity higher up the scale. This is quite enough to form the basis of a workable religion, without any of the trappings which have been added to it. It also resembles in a remarkable degree the teachings about Krishna and Arjuna found in the *Bhagavad-Gita*; for, of course, if all religions taught the exact truth they would all be exactly the same. There can only be one Truth; but the glimpses of it provided by great teachers long ago have been so distorted by their professional followers that all look completely different today.

Jesus admitted that He was a king, but that His kingdom was higher up the scale. Again we are bothered by words, what did the word 'king' mean in this context? Well, the Herods were styled kings. They were native rajahs subordinate to Rome. They had private bodyguards and palaces; but did not in any way compare with the Emperor himself. He could remove them in a moment had he wished to do so. Therefore the word king itself does not imply that on a higher level Jesus was the supreme ruler of everything. There is probably no modern equivalent to the word. The picture, which remains from this seems to confirm the Hindu belief in avatars, entities from a higher mental level of vibration than the usual one, who are sent down to the earth level at uncertain intervals to encourage people living on that level. When in a human body on the earth, they are both sons of God and sons of Man. This appears to be the explanation of all the conflicting statements in the Gospels.

It surely explains too all the difficulties, heresies, scisms and the like which follow all attempts to make a coherent picture out of an imaginary interpretation. If the avatar were omnipotent, then surely everyone would believe in him at once and the whole world become a good and kindly place. Instead of that rival variations of beliefs pursued one another through the ages with fire and sword. Jesus realized this and said it would happen : 'I came not to send peace on earth but a sword'.

Of course I ought not to write this, directly under the windows of the yacht club as it were. But we started off to look for the sons of God and it has led us to this point. We will now have to see whether it is in any way possible to pull the whole study together; or whether it remains just a mixed bag of unanswerable conundrums.

Eleven

The editor, or editors, of the original book of Genesis sought to begin his work with the story of how the world was created and how man came to be on it. He was confronted with at least three traditional stories which may have been ages old already and he tried to fit them together. Very many centuries later a British ecclesiastic tried to do a similar thing. Geoffrey of Monmouth attempted to compile a history of Britain, fitting in all the traditional scraps of history which came his way. At the time these things were written down few people had enough education to do more than listen to results with awe at the learning of the authors. Yet today both look like clumsy attempts to write of the impossible. All you can do with them is to try to disentangle the original traditional stories from the mixtures, to see whether they make sense and tell anything of general interest. The editor of Genesis was much less imaginative than Geoffrey and wrote down his conflicting stories without comment. He did write sentences from one into those of another; but did not try to add names he happened to know against the wrong events. Fortunately Geoffrey did this so badly that it is often possible to see at once when he has done it.

The editor of Genesis on the other hand seems to have had a surprisingly wide knowledge. The introductory portion of the book appears to show a general astronomical and geological knowledge far in advance of that of medieval Europe. Why, for instance, was it said that man was the latest living being to appear on the scene, unless something was known about it? If the whole thing had been a complete fiction, one would have expected them to put man first.

When therefore Genesis begins to talk of the sons of God and their dealings with the daughters of men, one begins to puzzle over what this could possibly refer to. It seems to be completely divorced from the story of Adam and Eve and one sees that there must be something we do not know about. Who, too, was God talking to when He said: 'Let us make man in our own image'? On the face of it, one would suppose that there was not one God, but a number of equals. Stranger still, this comes from a Hebrew writer and the Hebrews were the great advocates of a single god in a world which in general believed in many.

Perhaps the most remarkable bearing on the conflicting stories in Genesis is the truly amazing series of traditions extracted by a Polynesian from the Polynesian inhabitants of Easter Island, almost as remote a spot as you could find on the face of the globe. Here is a story of Adam and Eve almost identical with Genesis, coupled with a great deal of supposed information about the planets which could hardly have been derived from any modern source and does not look like spontaneous invention. A variant of the creation story of man being made out of clay and also several other figures being involved in this work is found also in ancient American Indian writings. It almost seems as if these creation stories were once spread all over the world, together with a great deal of information of an astronomical and geological nature. This is very odd indeed, for where could it possibly have spread from?

The general and quite rational idea has been that the sons of God were some people in antiquity who conquered whatever tribe it was who originated the Hebrew beliefs; but, in the present state of historical and archaeological knowledge, it is not easy to point to any conquerors who might fit the bill. Of course the Hebrews are supposed to have spent a long time in servitude in ancient Egypt and the Egyptians may have appeared very grand to them; but they can hardly have picked a single creator out of the mass of Egyptian gods and we know nothing in Egyptian literature comparable to the Easter Island traditions about the planets. That is not to say that there was no such information in Egypt; but it has not in that case survived the passage of time, although we might have expected the Greeks to have got hold of it.

Now a number of people today believe that the ancient civilization of Egypt was not a local product, but taken there by people from another planet. They point also to the occurrence of relatively similar civilizations in Egypt and Central America as proof of this. Others believe that the supposed lost island of Atlantis was the origin of both and that it in its turn was colonized from outside this earth. While there is no reason why we should take any of this very seriously, there is yet another hare running. Large numbers of people claim to have seen and to be seeing at frequent intervals vehicles in the skies, which had no origin on Earth. This is either denied or ignored by the responsible authorities throughout the world. Although I have had no personal experience of such things, yet such a large bulk of visual testimony has been collected and so many books published about it that one can hardly doubt that something has been frequently seen.

The explanation need not be correct; yet there must be one. It is not mass hysteria, for the eye-witnesses are seldom more than one or two at a time. Also, even supposing there are such things as these UFOs (flying saucers) there is no substantial link down the ages between them and the conjectural happenings of several thousand years ago. Over this very long interval of time, and if the visits had been on any comparable scale to those reported today, they must have been recorded by the competent observers of the Roman world. There are snippets here and there, which are taken to refer to such vehicles and we have tried to examine such stories, as that of Elijah without any noticeable success. The only place in the European area in which strong suggestions exist that there may at one time have been active visitors from elsewhere in our skies is to be found in the Greek myths and legends. These are very suggestive indeed and may have been of great antiquity when they came to be recorded. There are other possibilities in Indian writings; but whether these are to be trusted or not, we are still left with an enormous gap in time during which little seems to have happened at all.

Some confirmation of possible visitors long ago was found in a most unexpected and different problem. What was the purpose of the erection of stone and timber circles and stone alignments at the end of the Stone Age, in what is called the Megalithic Period? Here we took into consideration the relatively new study of bio-electronics, which is perhaps bio-magneto-electronics. Evidence was given that one at least of these circles, the Merry

Maidens, near Lamorna, in Cornwall, was still highly charged with this force. To attempt to explain this, evidence was found of the former and perhaps still existent belief of the west European witches that by performing excited ring dances they could store power in stones and trees. Nobody has told how they were supposed to get it out again; but it is known that at the time of the Spanish Armada the Hampshire witches met and sent a cone against the enemy ships, apparently producing the ensuing celebrated wind. Witches are always believed to be able to raise a storm. Experiments carried out by my wife and myself appeared to show that various bio-electronic elements could be forced into the electronic fields of beach pebbles and the same elements could be detected in the fields of sling-stones shot away more than two thousand years ago. It seems probable therefore that power generated by excited dancers could be stored in stone and tree circles and that this was permanent. Presumably the force detected at the Merry Maidens circle was of this nature.

It was then argued that since it can be shown that bio-electronic rays can apparently extend the whole way round the globe, those from stone or timber circles would extend upwards to a great height and that they could be detected from the sky by some relatively simple machine. The location of many of the circles in areas comparatively unimportant, except for metalliferous deposits, led to the perhaps wild suggestion that they could have been used as aerial navigational beacons, with a possible central base at the great megalithic collection of stone rows at Carnac in Brittany. Stonehenge, an apparently much more recent structure, did not seem to be part of this possible arrangement. Of course, this is entirely supposition.

The accepted belief among archaeologists is that such circles and alignments were for unknown religious purposes, probably connected with the burial of the dead. However, this is not entirely convincing and the religious ceremonies might be survivals from the original purpose of charging up the stones. There is a gap in our knowledge of why it was thought necessary to store power in stones or trees at all. Yet we have had striking evidence that it was done and in some cases that the power is still there, improbable though it undoubtedly is.

If all circles were connected with burial, then it might perhaps be thought that the purpose was to revive the dead; but it is not so. In such a state of lack of knowledge, it is then reasonable at least to think about any other possibility, however unlikely it may seem to be.

The way in which the stones were charged is no longer difficult to explain in a scientific manner, thanks to the able work of P. Callagan in America. He showed when studying the feeding and mating habits of moths that the heat engendered by the vibration of their wings produced a bio-electronic ray. This ray was used to contact either the moth's food supply or the female of the species. I found that precisely similar effects could be studied with a dowsing pendulum in the case of beetles. From this it is not very hard to see that the heat engendered by numerous excited human bodies, dancing in a ring with interrupted spacing of stones around it, could act as a human dynamo. The purpose then of the ritual dancing was to store this bio-electronic current. If there is any truth in the hypothesis that the ring was to be used as the equivalent of an electronic beacon, there would be no question of ever extracting the power; although it might need seasonal renewal. The practical purpose of the dance would in time, by frequent repetition, slowly change into a ritual one; of which the original cause was no longer remembered, if it was ever known. We can see then why, especially in Cornwall, terrible supernatural disaster was believed to follow the damage to a circle, or the removal of the stones. The original dancers had been told that this would happen and a belief in it was handed down as long as the dances were continued and even afterwards.

Of course, I am well aware that this is so tenuous as to be hardly worthy of mention; yet so was the original question. We could hardly expect to find an answer to 'Who were the sons of God?' The whole study is no more than a series of guesses and suppositions. As long as nobody believes that it is a terribly serious and important matter, no harm is done in speculation. How incredibly boring the world would be if you never let your imagination have its head at all. You would have even to take the fantastic promises of politicians as if they meant something, and as to the pronouncements of this or that professor on the television, why these would be the equivalent of the 'word of God'. So what I have said about these stone circles is no more than one guess out of many possibles. At the same time there is no need to believe that anybody knows a better answer.

The same holds good about the extraordinary collection of stone statues on Easter Island. Nobody knows why such infinite trouble was taken to cover a remote island with huge and exotic figures. One guesses that this was not done so very long ago, in the last thousand years at any rate. Is it possible that Easter Island was a point aimed at by a much later expedition of men from outside the earth and this is why the present inhabitants have such a curious collection of garbled information about other planets? It is just possible. It might mark the first stage of a new exploratory phase which had been discontinued for perhaps three thousand years. Why, for instance, was 'mana' required in the erection of the statues?

The interval of time between the setting up of the monuments in the Megalithic Period and the possible manifestation on Easter Island, brings up the second question of what was the war in heaven? If the Megalithic monuments could be used as evidence of the coming of explorers from space, then something happened to interrupt the operation. This is where I introduced my fairy tale of a possible war between two other planets, resulting in the devastation of Mars and the moon. Time may show whether there is any possibility of truth behind the fairy tale. But we know that for some time now various writers have been drawing attention to accounts of what might possibly have been fission bombs in ancient Indian writings. I do not know enough about this to comment and have not read the Indian material. Still, any clue of this sort might fit into the imaginary picture. Why does the Bible mention a war in heaven at all? It is such an unlikely thing for anyone to have mentioned in such a matter of fact way, that I am almost persuaded to believe that there was a genuine tradition of such a war. If there was one, it would explain the time gap.

There is another point to consider too. If the visits stopped because of the war in heaven, then the probability is that the visitors were losers. Their expeditions were cut off from home and eventually merged in the native population. It seems most likely that if flying saucers indeed come from space, then they are not from the original planet which lost the war. The earlier vehicles need not have been anything like saucers, but more like the present day rockets and capsules. The whole business may be about to start again and the visitors, instead of being faced with the exploration of a new world in an almost virgin state, find one with a technology not so very far behind their own. It would not confront them with a simple process of annexation and exploitation, but with the possibility of a long and desperate war. No wonder that they would have to look at it for a long time before deciding what to do.

Another suggestion has been that the saucers might be time machines from the earth's own future time, containing visitors from our own future, coming back in time to investigate their past. This idea, although apparently possible by making use of another level of vibration, would exclude the possibility of anyone landing from these machines without returning at once to their own time. Visitors from the future could not then be the sons of God who married the daughters of men. Attractive though the idea may be, it does not fit into our picture at all.

A third possibility pictures men living on the higher level itself, beyond the point of what we call death, experimenting with machines to enable them to watch what was happening on earth. Since these would be in a different plane altogether, no one without some degree of mediumistic powers would be able to see them. Therefore they cannot explain the Bible reference.

Lastly there is a class of beings known as avatars who apparently on rare occasions do come down from a considerably higher level of existence and are born for a life on earth. From all accounts these could well be spoken of as sons of God, but they do not conform at all to the behaviour of the sons of God mentioned in Genesis. They do not produce giants and warriors, but rather the reverse, being religious teachers of a high order. These avatars do not seem to be the answer to our question.

I may have overlooked something fundamental in all this and my reasoning from what I have considered may be quite unreliable. However, although everything is so faint and long ago as to be almost indiscernible, there does seem to be a residue of tradition which could make sense if we hit on the right interpretation. There is nothing in the records which would not fit in had there been experimental landings from elsewhere on earth, perhaps five thousand years ago, and if people from these explorations had been cut off from wherever they came from. I have not yet reached a stage in which I can believe that this did actually happen. Far from it, I feel it is all most improbable. But I do see that it could be a possible explanation of many things in ancient records and modern research which are at present completely disconnected. Such things as lost Atlantis and Mu would have their place in it, together with the mythical gods of Greece and those of many races. The mystery of why men built the Megaliths would be explained and our strange questions from the Bible at least partly answered.

But should this explanation be even partly correct, it could alter much that many people take for granted. Five thousand years ago at any rate there would have to have been people living somewhere else who were so like human beings on earth that they could intermarry with them and produce fertile offspring. They must have been of the same species as ourselves. Apparently the Russians already think along these lines and many people do in America.

The effect of this on the present widespread belief in the equality of man would be drastic. There would be two strains and not one. The quality of a given individual would depend on how much, if any, foreign blood he had in him and the foreign blood would probably be of a higher strain than the native. Since history records that in many lands there were determined attempts to restrict interbreeding among the ruling classes, this may well indicate that the earlier cross-breeds regarded their foreign admixture so highly that they looked on themselves as sons of the Gods. Although there must have been many lapses from these rules, there surely cannot have been enough time for the whole population of the world to have become blood relations. Of course, you can apparently prove anything with figures, but common sense indicates that such a complete mixing is most unlikely. If you accept the idea of the addition of foreign blood at all, then everything points to the establishing of more cultured warrior castes here and there all over the world and that these have not yet by any means completely broken down. The only reason then for the appearance of outstanding individuals here and there in the rest of the population would be the theoretical naughtiness of the young men of the warrior castes.

Once at a conference I heard the late Lord Raglan, the anthropologist, remark, to the horror of his audience: 'The labourer never invented anything at all.' At once there were cries of : 'Who did then?' 'The man who put the labourer to work,' replied Raglan imperturbably. We can see that this might very well have been true. The other man had the leisure to think.

It seems to me that this segregation, broken since the days of Alfred more frequently in England than in the rest of Europe, is an additional argument in favour of our fairy tale having some possible foundation in fact. Why, too, were the Aryans in India so set on keeping apart from the peoples they found there before them? This appears to be something more than an early knowledge of selective breeding.

Therefore with the greatest caution I think we can assume that there is a case for examination. Far back in time, beyond the hazy ghosts of long-forgotten swamps and forests, strange human figures from space may have arrived on earth to explore it and perhaps make arrangements for future colonization. Here, while busy on their survey work, they may have been cut off by disaster at home and eventually forced to become earth men. If one thinks of the normal composition of an exploring team, there would have been few among them with a practical knowledge of the techniques which had built up their industries at home and so their early efforts at metal working and such like activities would of necessity have been primitive. As a child I tried to cast my own lead toy soldiers without proper knowledge of how to do it. I did produce recognizable figures which would stand up, but they were very rough. The earliest copper axes and knives found by archaeologists remind me of my childhood's efforts and are the kind of things which might have been produced by men who knew that copper could be melted from its ores and made into tools, but did not know the technique and had to build it up from their own imagination. It is hard to see otherwise how metal working could have been invented by chance. It is perhaps easier to think that some unknown 'God' appeared from the sky and taught men how to do it. Easier perhaps, but not very much easier, for you are only pushing it further back on to another world in another age.

However, support comes from archaeology in rather a positive manner. The setters up of the stone circles, the Megalithic men, had no metal. Shortly afterwards copper appears in early forms of tools and a completely new breed of men is seen in Europe.

This type, generally spoken of as 'Beaker' man, was very unlike the slight, long-headed, oval-faced man of the Megaliths. Such examples as I have excavated were broad-shouldered, stocky individuals, of great muscular development and with heads as round as footballs. Some groups of these, using sturdy ponies, were clearly nomadic herdsmen and came to the west of Europe apparently from the skirts of the Alps. But little is really known of their origin. Whether they pushed down into the Biblical lands also, I have no idea. It is not easy to dig out such information from archaeological reports and I have not the time to attempt it. But in Europe at any rate the two types of men are so completely different in physical appearance as to suggest absolutely separate origins.

When you see burial mounds dotting the countryside, you think what a lot of Beaker men there must have been; yet in all probability their numbers at any one time were not great. Without a long and careful study it is impossible to form a reasonable guess; still, I fancy, that in one year you would not have found more than two or three thousand in the whole of Britain. If these men were our hypothetical half-breeds, then perhaps a few hundred years could have produced that number. There is very little to go upon and it is entirely guesswork. Still, where did this round head-shape come from? Could it possibly have been the normal shape on Mars?

As I said at the beginning, I am only putting up questions to most of which there is no known answer. I do not believe in the answers I have put forward, except to a very limited degree. For instance I do think that I have got right the method by which the bluestones were transported to Stonehenge. But I hope that it will provoke enough interest for others to try to solve some of the problems which are too difficult for me to answer.

It is not unimportant, for much theory is based on the assumption that there is only one kind of human being on one single planet. If it should be presently demonstrated that several planets have had the same species living on them, it must have a considerable effect on their thinking. If beyond that it could be shown that human beings from another planet had once landed here and mingled with the native species, one would tend to look at other members of our community with a questioning eye. 'Is that man a son of God?' It is improbable that many people would think it of any of our present day politicians, although many girls would believe it of their current young man.

However, if by some remote chance all this should happen to be correct, it is nothing to laugh about as I have just done. It must mean that five thousand years ago there were people somewhere else, far more advanced than we are today, who were able to explore our earth when its inhabitants were in the Stone Age. Something happened to the parent world of these explorers which prevented their return. This must in all probability have been a devastating war. It may have been with another planet, or the kind of thing which might now happen between two power blocks on earth. It was so destructive that it has taken five thousand years before one or other of the contestants has been in a position to do much about exploring earth again. When they do begin to do so, they find that the remote descendants of their original exploring parties, or those of their enemy, have developed that world to a technological condition not very far below their own level. They much desire to gain access to its resources, for their own are largely used up. Yet unless they could mount an expedition of overwhelming strength or very great skill, they know that it would be destroyed. What are they to do? After much examination and prolonged thought, they might even try a friendly approach, for a warlike one could make it uninhabitable for hundreds of years and there are probably traditions still remembered of the frightful results of the original war. Therefore there is probably little danger of an invasion of earth from the skies. In any case this is all imagination and we do not really know what unidentified flying objects may be : ghosts, hallucinations, time machines or honest to God visitors from another planet. Whatever they may be, they offer us an interesting subject for talk and speculation and the answer may come sooner than anyone expects.

I shall finish now. Many people will think it is all rubbish. Others will see some sense in it, even if I have produced no hard and fast theory. At least I hope I have given a few something to turn over in their minds, to see whether they can produce anything more satisfactory than I have been able to do.